Schneider

This book belongs to:

About the Author

Jim Brosnan was a professional baseball pitcher from 1947 to 1963, playing in the majors for the Cincinnati Reds and the Chicago White Sox. Since retiring from baseball, he has become a free-lance writer and a radio and television sportscaster. He is the author of *Great Baseball Pitchers* and *Great Rookies of the Major Leagues* (Little League Library #3 and #6), plus two adult books.

Photograph credits: Vernon J. Biever, 38, 136, 145; Rich Clarkson, cover (middle left), 124, 128, 131, 132; Malcolm W. Emmons, cover (bottom left), back end-paper, 2, 16, 42, 47, 146, 158; Curt Gunther, 135; Ken Regan, cover (top left and top right), 28, 34, 49, 52, 66, 82, 84, 100, 106; Fred Roe, 111; Suzanne Szasz, front end-paper; U.P.I., vi-vii, 4, 8, 11, 14, 21, 24, 40, 62, 63, 64, 68, 88, 103, 114, 116, 139, 150, 155, 160; Wide World, cover (bottom right), x, 72, 76–77, 93, 113, 121, 122, 143, 165.

Little League to Big League

Absorbing sketches of fourteen stars in five different sports who have in common their experiences as Little Leaguers. Included are: Carl Yastrzemski, Sam McDowell, Mike Ditka, Fran Tarkenton, Bill Bradley, Joey Jay, Ron Santo, Rich Nye, Roger Maris, Don Schollander, Jim Ryun, Steve Spurrier, Bill Freehan and Tommy John.

Little League to Big League

By Jim Brosnan

Illustrated with photographs

RANDOM HOUSE · NEW YORK

Little League Baseball is greatly pleased to join with Random House in the establishment of a Little League Library. It is our confident belief that the books thus provided will prove entertaining and helpful for boys of Little League age and indeed for their parents and all who are Little Leaguers at heart.

This is one of a series of official Little League Library Books. Each has been read and approved at Little League Headquarters. We hope they will bring enjoyment and constructive values to all who may have the opportunity of reading them.

P J Mc Govern

President and Chairman of the Board
Little League Baseball, Incorporated

Library of Congress Catalog Card Number 68-14486

Manufactured in the United States of America.

Contents

Introduction • xi

1. Carl Yastrzemski *The Reluctant Leader* • 3

2. Sam McDowell *Echoes of Sandy Koufax* • 17

3. Mike Ditka *The Hammer* • 29

4. Fran Tarkenton *A Peach of a Passer* • 39

5. Bill Bradley *The Making of a Superstar* • 53

6. Joey Jay *The Head of the Class* • 69

7. Ron Santo *Hard-Nosed Hustler* • 81

8. Rich Nye *Mod-Style Moundsman* • 89

9. Roger Maris *The New King of Swat* • 101

10. Don Schollander *The Machine* • 115

11. Jim Ryun *Running Is Fun!* • 125

12. Steve Spurrier *Goldflinger* • 137

13. Bill Freehan *Iron Man with a Golden Glove* • 147

14. Tommy John *Mathematician on the Mound* • 159

Index • 170

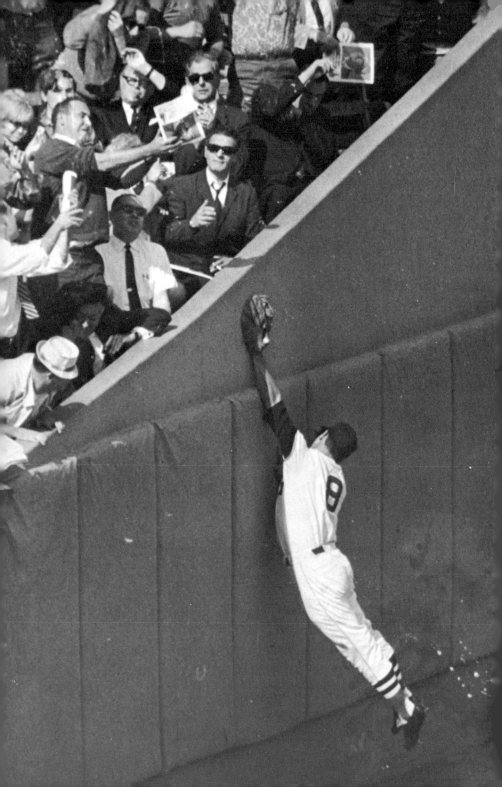

Introduction

Baseball is an easy game to learn. Most American boys play it in one form or another, including hardball, softball and stickball. Also, baseball can be played almost anywhere—at ball parks, with umpires to call the game, or on corner lots or in the streets.

For the last generation, Little League, Inc. has been the leader in organizing baseball teams for young boys. According to the directors of Little League, "organized play activity trains boys in teamwork, sportsmanship, discipline and character building." Little League programs may or may not build better citizens for the community, but at their best these programs can develop better athletes for a variety of big league sports.

For example, consider outstanding major league pitchers Joey Jay and Sam McDowell, and slugging outfielders Roger Maris and Carl Yastrzemski. Each learned to play baseball in Little League. Track star Jim Ryun, basketball marvel Bill Bradley, and pro football's finest tight end, Mike Ditka, also played Little League baseball.

For the budding ballplayer Little League offers certain permanent values: early training, proper mental and physical preparation and youthful enthusiasm. Yastrzemski, Bradley, McDowell and Ditka learned something useful from their Little League competition. Of course, not every boy can become a sports star. Ambitious dreams can't transform an uncoordinated youth into a champion athlete. In most cases champions are *born* with exceptional ability.

But training in basic fundamentals is necessary for success in any sport. Good habits learned early give an athlete reflexes he can depend upon later.

"It's the little things that count," says Don Schollander, the swimming perfectionist who won four gold medals at the 1964 Olympic Games. "I learned one thing in Little League. Get the details down pat and the results will speak for themselves."

Proper coaching is also necessary for a potential big leaguer. The advantage of organized play activity lies in the counseling of the adult group leader. A good coach explains not only how but why his boys should play the game properly.

"I was taught early," says Sam McDowell, "that the only way to win in life, as well as in baseball, is to work hard for what you want."

Champion athletes work hard, in practice and in

competition. The boy athlete who quits when the game is no longer fun seldom makes the big leagues. The sooner he learns to play his best at all times, the sooner he gets to the top.

A champion athlete must also possess enthusiasm for his sport. He can't win all the time, so he must enjoy competition for its own sake. Tough competition frightens many young boys, but the willingness to compete is vital to an athlete. Mike Ditka believes that the sense of competition must be acquired at an early age.

"You can't learn it later on," he says. "I was lucky to be on a good team when I was a boy, so playing was fun. The challenge to be the best keeps you going out for more."

Critics of Little League baseball claim that the importance of winning is overemphasized and that the influence of organized sports at an early age can be harmful. They feel that youngsters should play baseball only for fun. Furthermore, they say, parents often become unnecessarily involved and tend to push their boys too hard. As Roger Maris explains the problem, too many parents want their Little Leaguers to be *big* leaguers.

Obviously, winning is all-important in the big leagues, but having fun and learning to play the game well should be the most important aspects of Little League activity—to the boys and their parents alike.

Most of the big leaguers whose stories appear on the following pages were enthusiastic about their Little League experiences. Only Joey Jay, the first Little Leaguer to pitch in the majors, considers Little League more harmful than helpful.

In one sense, all the stars in this book owe their later successes to lessons they learned as boys. And Little League was a valuable source of experience for them, as well as for thousands of other boys who never went on to athletic fame.

Little League to Big League

1.
CARL YASTRZEMSKI
The Reluctant Leader

In the world of major league baseball, stars come in many shapes, sizes and dispositions. For example, the celebrated outfielders Mickey Mantle, Frank Robinson and Carl Yastrzemski all represent a totally different type of player. Mantle is endowed with a big, muscular and perfectly proportioned body. At the peak of his career, he ran like a sprinter and hit home runs out of sight. His teammates claim that they play better simply because he is in the same line-up. In other words, Mantle is a natural team leader.

Frank Robinson is tall but ungainly. His powerful torso is supported by legs as spindly as a stork's. He has a rough, needling sense of humor that irritates as many as it amuses. Yet, twice in five years, Robinson has driven his clubs to league pennants: Cincinnati, in 1961; Baltimore, in 1966.

Carl Yastrzemski is no bigger than the average baseball fan. His personality is agreeable but quiet. He is neither a leader nor a pusher. Still, it would be inaccurate to say that he is a follower. He is a lone star, one who stands out as a splendid individualist.

When he first joined Boston in the spring of 1961, Yastrzemski was called the best rookie prospect to come up to the majors since Mickey Mantle. He was known as the "Sensation of the Sixties," and reporters often compared him to Stan Musial because Carl's line-drive style was similar. *The Sporting News,* an authority in baseball circles, virtually conceded Rookie-of-the-Year honors to Yastrzemski.

Boston fans saw in Yastrzemski a genuine suc-

Yastrzemski receives batting tips from Ted Williams.

cessor to the great Ted Williams. Williams, another outstanding individualist, had retired in the fall of 1960 after establishing a record as one of the finest hitters in baseball history. Watching Yastrzemski in batting practice the next spring, Williams said, "The boy has everything. Poise. A good eye. A smooth stroke."

Yastrzemski eventually fulfilled Williams' predictions and became a superb outfielder and a strong, consistent hitter. He was obviously cut out to be a star. Yet, from the beginning of his career with the Red Sox he puzzled fans and experts alike because he was a star who seemed unable to inspire his team.

Yastrzemski's ability to play baseball had always impressed people. As a Little Leaguer, playing for the Bridgehampton Lions, in Long Island, Carl had pitched as well as he hit.

"I'd pitch nine innings a week," he recalls. "Strike out eighteen or nineteen batters. I threw this big roundhouse curve ball. It would seem to be heading for a spot behind the batter's back. Then it would break over the plate and really scare him."

However, throwing too many curves hurt Carl's arm. In his sophomore year in high school, he had to give up pitching and move to the outfield.

"I couldn't even pick up a ball that year," says Yastrzemski. "I was very fortunate that my arm came back later on. Of course, a sore arm never hurt my hitting."

Yastrzemski batted over .500 in high school and, as a result, every club in the major leagues was eager to obtain his services. The Cincinnati Reds offered him $100,000, but he turned them down. The Milwaukee Braves (prior to moving to Atlanta) gave him a special workout and were so impressed that they offered him a bonus of $115,000. He turned them down, too, because Milwaukee was too far from home.

Finally, when the Red Sox agreed to pay his way through Notre Dame, as well as put $100,000 in his bank account, Yastrzemski turned pro. In his first season, at Raleigh in the Carolina League, Carl hit .377 and won the batting title by 66 points.

Promoted to Minneapolis, then a member of the American Association, Carl batted .339 and was named Rookie-of-the-Year in Class AAA baseball. One frustrated opposing manager said:

"We pitched him up. We pitched him down. We went in, we went out. We jammed him. Used slow curves. He still killed us."

In a way, Yastrzemski was a victim of advance notices in 1961. Ted Williams had predicted that Carl would hit .320 as a rookie big leaguer. In his first official appearance in the American League, Yastrzemski lined a single to left field. Later in the week he belted a long triple to right center. But two years of minor league experience were not quite enough to sustain him against seasoned professionals. His batting stroke, which was naturally smooth, needed major league polish, and he hit only .266 during his first season. However, Yastrzemski led the league with 12 assists. And even his critics admitted that the rookie left fielder was one of the best defensive players that Boston had seen in a long time.

Still, it was not until mid-May of 1962 that Yastrzemski's star began to shine brightly. For the last two-thirds of the 1962 season, Carl batted over .300. He also hit 19 homers and batted in 94 runs. To Red Sox fans, it seemed only a matter of time before "Yaz" would lead them to the promised land of the first division.

In 1963 Yastrzemski led the American League in hitting. He batted .321 and belted 40 doubles, a league-leading mark. Fellow players in the league voted him to the All-Star team. His future success seemed assured.

Unfortunately, Yastrzemski's teammates were not ready for better things. There was a noticeable lack of team spirit among the Red Sox. Yastrzemski himself was accused by his manager, Johnny Pesky, of "not putting out a hundred percent." Carl later excused the bad attitude of Red Sox players as frustration caused by tension.

Yaz slides into third as the Cards' Mike Shannon waits for the throw.

"There's always this bad tension on a losing team," said Yastrzemski. "Playing with second division teams that never cared has almost killed me."

Yastrzemski's failure to become a full-fledged star was due mostly to the poor performances of his teammates, but he was partly responsible himself. He once admitted to sports writer Mark Mulvoy that he played like a spoiled brat during his first six seasons with Boston. Still, no matter how well he played, the Red Sox were just as bad as before, and he was prevented from enjoying his own success. Naturally, when he was unfairly blamed for the team's failure, he resented it.

In 1965, Yastrzemski's new manager, Billy Herman, tried harder to understand the young star.

"Yaz wants to do well so badly," said Herman. "He wants to be the best at everything, every time. At golf, at cards, at bowling."

Yastrzemski flourished under Herman's leadership. He got off to a great start, hitting the ball with more power than he had ever shown before. In mid-season, however, he injured one of his kidneys by sliding into a base. Hospitalized for eight days, he returned to the line-up and immediately suffered a pulled thigh muscle.

Yastrzemski played in only 133 games in 1965, but his slugging percentage led the league. His hits included 20 home runs (a career high) and 45 doubles (which gave him a tie for the league lead).

In the spring of 1966, manager Herman named him captain of the Red Sox. Herman hoped to perk up his moody slugger and make him become a team leader. Yastrzemski accepted the title, but he didn't like the responsibility that went with it.

"I didn't really want to be captain," he said later. "I had my own problems. Everybody with a gripe came to me. I worried more about them than about my hitting."

That year Yastrzemski's batting average dipped to .278, the worst since his rookie season. Rumors that the Red Sox were seriously considering trading him were a shock to Carl. He had just built a $75,000 house in Lynnfield, Massachusetts. Not wishing to be uprooted from his home because he had failed his team, Yastrzemski was determined to make a comeback that would force the Red Sox to accept him once again.

After the conclusion of the 1966 season a physio-therapist suggested that he go into training to build himself up for the coming season. Following this advice, Yastrzemski pursued a daily, 90-minute muscle-toning program all winter long. In spring training, 1967, he was a changed man. To Boston's new manager, Dick Williams, he said:

"I'll do anything you tell me. I just want this club to have a good year."

Immediately Williams told him that he was no longer team captain.

"There are no captains on my club," said Williams. "I'm the only chief. The rest of you are Indians."

Freed from the worrisome responsibility, Yas-trzemski went on a batting rampage when the season opened. In his first 33 games, he drove in 25 runs. The tough off-season conditioning had increased his strength and sharpened his reflexes and coordination.

"All of a sudden I found I could pull pitches better than ever," said Carl. "Even outside fast balls. I started pulling all the time."

American League pitchers who thought they knew how to handle Yaz were perplexed by his new power stroke. Once again he was voted an All-Star by American League players. Some American

Teammates congratulate Yastrzemski after he has hit his 44th
home run.

League managers, however, were reluctant to acknowledge his increasing maturity. Eddie Stanky, the manager of the Chicago White Sox, said:

"He's an All-Star from the neck down."

In his next appearance against Chicago, during a double-header at White Sox Park, Yastrzemski replied to Stanky's remark by getting six hits in nine at-bats. One of the hits was a long home run. The entire Red Sox bench applauded as Yaz rounded the bases. As he touched third, he tipped his hat to Stanky in the Chicago dugout.

Returning to Boston, Yastrzemski gave Red Sox fans an encore, slugging two more homers and making two sensational catches. The crowd of 25,000 fans gave him a standing ovation.

But in contrast to past seasons, Yastrzemski's performance was being matched by his teammates. For the first time in years, Boston was in the first division when the two leagues got together for the All-Star game. It was soon apparent that the Red Sox were there to stay.

Yastrzemski starred in the field as well as at bat. During one mid-July double-header in Boston he threw out four base runners. And with the help of those assists the Red Sox won each game. Billy Martin, coach of the Minnesota Twins, called Yastrzemski "the best left fielder I ever saw!"

On August 1, Yastrzemski led the club in hits, home runs, runs batted in, doubles, total bases, runs scored and walks. During a streak of hits and walks, he had reached base safely in 56 successive games. He was on his way to doubling his career high in home runs, and he even threatened Ted Williams' record for homers hit by a Red Sox left-hander.

The 1967 pennant race drew to a furious close in September. Four clubs—Boston, Chicago, Minnesota and Detroit—occupied first place at one time or another during that final month. Newspapers all over the country were calling 1967 "The Year of The Great Race." In Boston, fans put it more simply. It was "The Year of the Yaz."

All season long Yastrzemski had blazed the trail for the Red Sox. Although critics called Boston the least of the four contenders, Carl and the Sox refused to believe them. In Boston's last 12 games Yastrzemski put on a spectacular show with his bat. The Red Sox won eight of those critical contests as Yaz collected 23 hits in 44 at-bats, an average of .523. He hit five home runs, drove in 16 runs and scored 14.

In a climactic weekend series with Minnesota, Boston had to win both games to clinch the pennant. During the series, Yastrzemski got a total of seven hits in eight times at bat. In Saturday's game he hit his 44th homer to win the game. On Sunday his four hits helped Boston to wrap up the pennant. In addition to his batting performance on Sunday, he cut down a Minnesota runner with a perfect throw from the left-field corner.

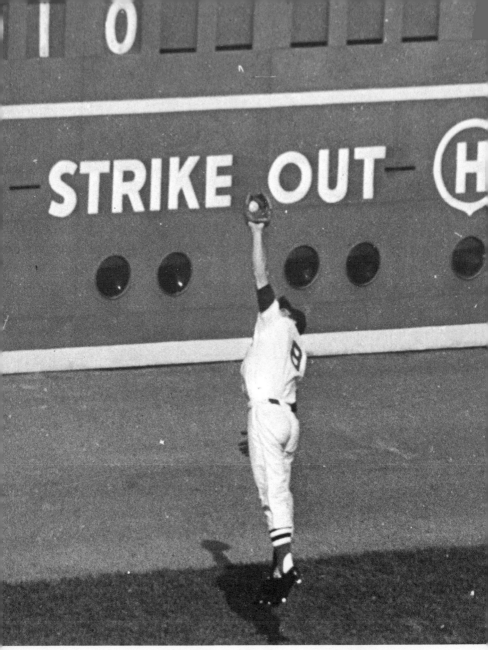

Yastrzemski makes a spectacular catch during the first game
of the 1967 World Series against the Cardinals.

With this last explosive performance Yastrzemski finished the season leading the league in seven offensive departments: Batting Average—.326; Runs Batted In—121; Runs Scored—112; Total Hits— 189; Total Bases—360; Slugging Percentage—.622; and a tie with Minnesota's Harmon Killebrew for Most Home Runs—44. His monopoly on the offensive records that season brought him baseball's Triple Crown.

One American League manager summed up Yastrzemski's performance for 1967:

"He's got to be the Most Valuable Player in the league," said Gil Hodges of the Washington Senators. "What more can a guy do?"

The 1967 Red Sox were best of their class, and their success was sparked by the example of a player who didn't really think of himself as a leader. But the Red Sox knew better.

2.
SAM McDOWELL
Echoes of Sandy Koufax

"I don't know how I strike out batters," says Sam McDowell. "If someone told me to do it I wouldn't know where to begin."

In 1965, at the age of 22, Sam McDowell struck out 325 American League batters. His total was just 23 short of Bob Feller's league record. Although McDowell wasn't sure how he achieved his strikeout total, the sluggers who played for the Yankees, Red Sox, Tigers and Twins were able to bear witness to his effectiveness. When Sam fired his fast ball he made even good hitters look bad. To the teams who played against the Cleveland Indians when "Sudden Sam" was on the mound, he often seemed untouchable.

Among big league pitchers an extraordinary fast ball is often called "the great hummer." Feller threw one. So did Walter Johnson, Dizzy Dean and Sandy Koufax. Sam McDowell seemed to have the same talent.

In 1966, however, Sam McDowell's great hummer

became a thing of the past. American League batters wondered what had happened to it. Often they would prepare themselves for McDowell's vaunted fast ball, but instead he would give them a slow change-up pitch. Sam threw wide curves and many neat little sliders, but the question was, why didn't he fire his fast ball?

The reason was that he didn't have faith in it any more.

"If I tried to get by with just my fast ball I'd get killed," said Sam.

But slugger Frank Howard held a contrary opinion:

"Any time Sam throws something besides a fast ball he's doing you a favor."

"Sam won't believe in his best stuff!" cried Del Crandall, the veteran catcher who had been hired to help McDowell. In Crandall's 15-year big league career he had seen few other pitchers with Sam's talent. He had batted against Koufax. He had caught for Bob Veale, the fireballing left-hander of the Pittsburgh Pirates. He was awed by Sam McDowell's ability, but he couldn't convince him to use his best pitch.

"Sam likes to be a do-it-yourself pitcher," explained Crandall. "He wants to call the game himself. All a catcher can do is make suggestions. You have to ask Sam if he wants to pitch your way or his way. Fortunately he's got enough talent to do it his way and get away with it."

McDowell's record in 1965 had led to predictions that he, not Sandy Koufax, would be the best left-handed pitcher in baseball. Many people said that McDowell was faster than Koufax. They admitted that Sandy had a great curve ball, but said that McDowell had *two* good curves, one short and sharp, the other big and round.

Koufax, moreover, had chronic arthritis in his pitching arm, and he was past the prime years of his baseball life. At 22 McDowell was just old enough to vote, and he had six years to go before he reached what baseball experts call a "physical peak."

Sam McDowell was a baseball celebrity even in his Little League days. Sam was a native of Pittsburgh, Pennsylvania, and he pitched for the Merchants of Morningside, a Little League team managed by his father. As Sam recalls:

"I won forty-one games, lost eleven, and batted .329 during the five years I played Little League ball. And everything I've learned in the majors later on my Dad had already told me back then."

As a pitching star at the age of nine, Sam set some fantastic records. He hurled 40 no-hitters before he graduated from high school. In his senior year at Pittsburgh's Central Catholic High, Sam didn't allow a single earned run all season.

"It was Little League that taught me not only

how to win in baseball but in life," says Sam. "You have to work for it. To begin with, you have an asset which you can utilize to become a star. Stardom won't be given to you, though. You have to work for it."

To young Sam baseball was fun, as well as rewarding.

"I used to loaf with the boys on the corner having what *they* called fun. But it was always the same old thing. I wanted excitement and I found it in baseball. They made fun of me whenever I had to play instead of loaf with them. Now those boys are out looking for jobs. I'm out looking too, only I'm out looking for things to buy with the money I made playing baseball."

McDowell's teen-age dedication and achievements were nothing to laugh about. Every major league team except the Dodgers took him seriously. Their offers of a contract plus bonus money were particularly welcome; for after the Cleveland Indians gave Sam a bonus of $62,000 to become a professional, he bought a house for his parents and a car for himself.

To the Indians, such a large amount was not really a high price to pay for an 18-year-old whose scouting report read in part:

"Possibly one of the great pitchers in the game, if he is able to handle himself and mature."

Sam spent the summer of 1960 at Lakeland,

Florida, where he fanned 100 batters in 105 innings. Promoted to Salt Lake City the next year, he won 13, lost 10 and was recalled by Cleveland in September to pitch a game against Minnesota.

"Pitching in the minors was a waste of time," Sam says. "When I got up to the majors, though, I went to work."

Sam worked so hard in his debut against the Twins that he broke two ribs just throwing his fast ball.

In 1962 McDowell was wild on the mound and unrestrained off the field. He frightened opposing

McDowell starts for first base after connecting with the ball in a game against the Yankees.

batters and he puzzled his teammates. He walked as many batters as he struck out. And sports writers called him "flaky" because of his long sideburns and a cowboy outfit he wore when he wasn't pitching. Although his dedication to baseball flagged, his skill as a pool player sharpened. Still, the contradictions in his behavior simply reinforced the club's belief that, if he ever grew up, Sam McDowell would stand out.

In 1963 a sore arm hampered Sam's performance. He started the season in Cleveland and finished it in Jacksonville, Florida, playing in the International League. A winter's rest didn't help him much, though. At the 1964 Tucson training camp of the Indians, Sam said his arm was sore again. Later the Cleveland club shipped him to Portland in the Pacific Coast League.

Indian officials began to have second thoughts about McDowell's talent. Some said his sore arm was in his head. McDowell said he had had too much advice on how to pitch. And, as a result, he no longer felt comfortable on the mound.

At Portland, Manager Johnny Lipon tried a new approach with the tall fireballer. He let Sam have his own way.

"John didn't try to tell me anything about pitching," says Sam. "Pretty soon the soreness in my arm went away."

With his new strength and confidence, McDowell

made Pacific Coast League hitters seem like Little Leaguers. He won eight games in a row, pitched 35 consecutive scoreless innings and 17 consecutive *hitless* innings. The Indians recalled McDowell in late spring of 1964. He was finally ready for the big league.

In 1964 and 1965, McDowell pitched in 73 games for Cleveland. During those two years, he struck out a total of 502 American League batters. But in the same time he gave up 232 bases on balls. Fortunately, Sam was just wild enough to make hitters nervous at the plate, and he threw so hard that he made many wish they were somewhere else.

But McDowell wasn't satisfied with pure speed.

"Throwing fast balls all the time would make pitching a dull game," he said. "The dumbest thing I was ever told was to just rear back and fire."

Sam worked on his slider—a curve ball that looks like a fast ball until it gets near the plate, where (if thrown by a left-hander) it breaks sharply towards right-handed batters. Mel Parnell, a master of the slider when he pitched for Boston in the late 1940's, said that Sam's slider was as good as any he had ever seen.

"It breaks nearly eight inches, three times the average," Parnell observed. "Combined with Sam's hummer it ought to be devastating."

McDowell still wasn't happy. He wanted a big slow curve and a straight change-of-pace to upset

McDowell and catcher Del Crandall wait on the mound as Manager Birdie Tebbetts calls for a new pitcher.

his opponents' timing. American League batters were baffled. They were already upset every time Sam threw his fast ball.

When the 1966 season opened Sam got off to a fast start. He won his first four games, pitched two one-hitters, and caused the Cleveland club to think about the World Series. Sam's fast ball hummed, his slider crackled and his change-up was effective.

Then in three successive starts he lost control of himself. In a game with Washington he asked to be taken out because he thought that he had lost his rhythm. In another game the White Sox bombed him for five runs before he could retire a man. And in Detroit, working on a four-run lead in the second inning, he complained of a sore arm.

"In the first inning my arm hurt while throwing the curve," said Sam. "Then I couldn't use my slider in the second. So I had to get out of there before I got killed."

When someone pointed out that McDowell could probably defeat the Tigers with just his fast ball, Sam frowned. He wanted to be known as a complete pitcher, not just a hard thrower. He had developed a strong array of pitches and if he couldn't use them he wasn't going to pitch.

McDowell missed 15 starts because of the soreness in his arm. When he was picked to pitch in the All-Star Game, he refused the assignment.

"I lost my grip on things," he explained later. "I really thought I was going to let down the league. Just like I was letting down the club."

Although Cleveland's manager, Birdie Tebbetts, defended McDowell's unusual behavior, Sam's detractors were numerous. Early Wynn, the Indian pitching coach, said:

"You can never tell what's in Sam's head."

Sports writers severely criticized McDowell in the papers. Fans mailed him nasty letters. Sam brooded and hoped for better days. Occasionally, during the summer, the old flame was visible. In a game with California he pitched a two-hit shutout, fanned 13 batters and caused the Angels to moan:

"If that's a sore arm, all of our pitchers should hurt theirs!"

Later in the year, on September 18, Sam fanned nine of the first 10 Detroit batters he faced. He had never looked better and he felt that he had a chance to break Sandy Koufax's record of 18 strikeouts in one game. But on the bench he talked so much about how stiff his arm felt that George Strickland, who had replaced Tebbetts as manager, finally took him out at the start of the seventh. Sam was incensed.

"I could taste that record," he says. "I didn't want out of the game. I just wanted George to have somebody ready just in case."

McDowell's self-doubt irritated the Indian management. No one could convince him that he just had to endure some types of pain without complaining. No pitcher could expect to be in perfect health every time he pitched. Before Tebbetts was fired he had told Sam:

"If you want to be great and make a lot of money you have to pitch with pain."

Sam was contrite. He blamed himself for Tebbetts' dismissal. Had he been throwing his great hummer all year long, Sam thought, the Indians would probably have been fighting for the pennant and Birdie would have been a hero instead of a failure.

Still, McDowell led the league in strikeouts,

despite the soreness in his biceps. It was not a critical injury. The Indians hoped he would be able to live with the harsh facts of a pitcher's life and learn to work even when his arm hurt a little.

McDowell's failure to live up to expectations in 1966 took some of the pressure off him during the 1967 season. He was no longer subjected to an analysis every time he lost a game. Standing 6 feet 5 inches and weighing 220 pounds, he still had the smooth delivery that made hitters blink at his fast ball. Although he was wild and erratic at times, walking 123 batters, he fanned 236. His strikeout total put him in second place, behind league-leading Jim Lonborg of the pennant-winning Boston Red Sox.

McDowell was only 25 years old and he had yet to reach the prime of his career. In the back of his mind a nagging ambition kept him going.

"You're not a big leaguer," he once said, "until you win twenty games." Like Sandy Koufax, Sam McDowell was maturing slowly. But he showed every sign of becoming as great a pitcher in the big leagues as he had been in Little League.

3.
MIKE DITKA
The Hammer

For most of his life Mike Ditka has played football in one form or another. As boy and man, as amateur and professional, he has been a success. His impressive list of achievements includes: All-State fullback at Aliquippa High in Aliquippa, Pennsylvania; All-America linebacker at the University of Pittsburgh; and All-Pro offensive end with the Chicago Bears of the NFL. Throughout his career he has given people the impression that he is never quite satisfied with his performance as a player. He learned early that he possessed athletic ability, but he also discovered that he wanted to be better than his teammates. In fact, he wanted to be the best.

At the age of 11, Mike was the catcher for a Little League team sponsored by Plodnick's furniture store in Aliquippa.

"I even had ambitions to be a big league baseball player," Mike recalls. "But back in Little League they didn't throw curve balls! I learned about them later. But in 1952, when Plodnick's won the league championship, I was happy just playing the game.

"I've always enjoyed anything competitive. Those Little League games helped me a lot, just giving me a chance to compete. Winning is everything to you at that age. And it should be. You can't pick up competitiveness in later years."

As a sophomore at Aliquippa high school, Mike felt his first twinges of doubt about the worth of competing in organized sports. He weighed only 130 pounds, and although he loved the physical contact of football, he took such a beating in practice session that his mother thought he might be seriously injured.

"I liked to hit, and be hit, then hit 'em again harder," Mike says, "but things got to the point where I even thought about quitting. My high-school coach, who did as much for me as anybody in the world, talked me into staying with it."

In his junior year at Aliquippa, Ditka played offensive end and defensive linebacker for a team that won all of its games. In his senior year he became a fullback. Then, at the University of Pittsburgh, he returned to the end position on offense, while continuing as a linebacker on defense. As an end, he earned national recognition and won nearly all the awards a college lineman can receive. He was selected for a total of 11 All-America teams. But in spite of his numerous awards and honors, Mike did not take them too seriously.

"What do they mean? All-America! It's an honor, yes, but nothing to brag about. Some All-Americans can't even play pro ball!"

Ditka's determination to play with the best impressed every coach who worked with him. John Michelosen, head coach at the University of Pittsburgh, said:

"Mike was the most gung-ho player I ever coached. As a sophomore he used to be so wrung out after four minutes I'd have to take him out and give him a breather."

The end coach at Pittsburgh, Ernie Hefferle, once gave Ditka some advice that stuck in Mike's mind and became a guide for his future behavior:

"Let 'em know who you are!"

In college Ditka seldom was downed until he was buried by tacklers. He once carried a Notre Dame safety man on his back for 15 yards, a performance that brought Ditka a Lineman-of-the-Week award. Pro scouts who saw him that day sent back reports to their teams classifying him as prime material for the National Football League.

In practice sessions, Ditka would often pound his college teammates unmercifully. And in games he battered every opponent who got in his way. Later, as a rookie pro, Mike blocked so savagely and ran over defensive backs so often that Bill Wade, the Chicago quarterback, has always retained one vivid impression of him:

"I picture Mike with one hand on the ball, the other hand free, looking for someone to hit."

Mike's habit of bowling over everybody who got in his way on the gridiron prompted a sports writer to nickname him "The Hammer." At one time or another, Ditka has smashed blocking sleds in practice, plastic helmets during games, and opponents' bones on occasions when he could not avoid it.

Willie Davis, the outstanding defensive end of the Green Bay Packers, takes a wary but admiring view of Ditka:

"You know that Mike's going to punish you and

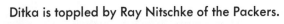

Ditka is toppled by Ray Nitschke of the Packers.

you'd better be prepared to punish him during a game. He likes it that way."

Ditka often receives as many bruises as he gives. During games, he has been stepped on, kicked, slugged and injured. But he accepts pain as part of the game, and this realistic attitude contributes to the image of toughness that teammates and opponents have of him.

"Pain?" says Mike. "I can take it. Depends on how much I want to play. And that goes for anybody. Both of the serious injuries I've had were freak happenings. But operations made me just as good as ever. Injuries are the farthest thing from my mind when I go into a game. If I ever lose that attitude then I'm done as a pro."

In his rookie year with the Bears Mike demonstrated both a savagely competitive attitude and a violent temper. He often delighted fans by hurling his helmet on the ground after a bad play. But some pros resented Mike for losing control of himself. Eventually Mike got the message:

"Whenever I lost my temper on the field I felt foolish. But I'm a guy who can't even stand to lose a game of Ping-Pong. If that kind of competitiveness seems ridiculous, I'm sorry. I don't see anything wrong with it."

Ditka's striving for perfection irritated some players who were happy simply to be wearing pro uniforms. Characteristically, Ditka responded to their resentment with an equal measure of irritation.

"There aren't too many people I don't like," he says, "but a guy who won't put out one hundred percent on the field is simply pitiful. He cheats himself and everybody connected with him."

Ditka's dedication to maximum effort led to his most memorable college game. During his senior year at Pitt, Mike was captain of the team. Just before the game with heavily favored Syracuse, he called a private meeting of his teammates and threatened the whole squad:

"If we get beat I'm gonna want to know why."

He didn't smile when he said it. Then the fired-up

Still holding the ball, Ditka gets up from a pile of tacklers.

Pitt team proceeded to wallop Syracuse University for the first time in 17 years.

Ditka's teammates on the Chicago Bears have characterized him as a fearlessly frank player, with an absolute commitment to winning. Mike Pyle, the veteran center, says:

"Ditka would call you down when you did wrong, compliment you when you did right. And he spoke up 'right now'! He didn't wait till after the game. Maybe you didn't like the criticism, but you respected him for it."

Bear quarterback Rudy Bukich had a great deal of respect for the big end who caught many of his passes:

"It was a pleasure to throw Mike the ball and watch him run over people."

In 1967, after expressing dissatisfaction over his contract with the Bears, Mike was traded to the Philadelphia Eagles. But, during his six years with Chicago, he had proved to be the best blocking end in the team's history. He had also developed into a superb pass catcher and scoring threat. Ironically, in college his coaches had had doubts about his ability to run pass patterns and to hold onto a ball once it hit his hands.

"When I went into the NFL," says Mike, "I found out I didn't know a thing about football. College ball is really not adequate preparation for the pro game. I knew I could block. But I had to practice catching passes. Billy Wade would throw all day if you asked him. And I did. And I got better."

Ditka's record for receptions with the Bears is a proud one. In 1961, after he had polished his technique with the aid of star pass-catcher Harlon Hill, Mike won Rookie-of-the-Year honors. He snatched 56 passes for 12 touchdowns and an average gain of 19 yards for each carry. Three years later, he caught 75 passes and gained a total of 897 yards. During his career in Chicago, he caught 316 passes for 34 touchdowns and a total gain of 4,503 yards.

Ditka's favorite performance with the Bears occurred during the 1963 NFL championship game against the New York Giants. Late in the third quarter, the Bears were on the New York 13-yard line. Wade called a quick "look-in" pass to Ditka. (A "look-in" is a play in which the quarterback straightens up immediately after taking the snap from the center and throws to an end or a flanker moving diagonally toward the area between the defensive ends or the corner linebackers.) The pass was completed for 12 yards and a first down on the one-yard line. On the next down, Wade dove into the end zone for the winning touchdown. The Bears won, 14–10, with Ditka making a key play.

"I tried to get 'em to call that pass on the third play of the game," said Ditka. "But I couldn't communicate with anybody. As a matter of fact, I had beaten my guy a couple of times during the game but the ball didn't get to me."

Ditka had worked hard to acquire his skills at running patterns and catching passes and he was annoyed when he couldn't put them to use.

"When I ran my patterns and beat my man I got mad if I didn't get the ball," he said.

In professional football, a first-class tight end has to outmaneuver and outbatter many opponents: giant tackles, big linebackers and little safetymen. He needs size, durability and speed to survive. Mike Ditka began his career with the necessary ability to play in big league sports; and to his physical ability he has added eagerness to accept the challenge of competition. Mike has hammered himself as hard as he has hammered opponents, and the result is pro football's finest tight end.

4.
FRAN TARKENTON
A Peach of a Passer

"That kid's going to get killed!" said Gino Marchetti. He was predicting Fran Tarkenton's future as a professional quarterback. Marchetti had just spent a Sunday afternoon in September, 1961, chasing the rookie quarterback of the Minnesota Vikings all around the gridiron. Marchetti's job as defensive end of the Baltimore Colts was to stop Tarkenton from passing.

Marchetti was an established star, a veteran pro who usually carried out his duties in less than five seconds, either tackling the quarterback or forcing him to pass. Tarkenton was a rookie playing with a first-year team in the National Football League. The Vikings were one of the "expansion teams" formed to increase the number of NFL teams throughout the country. Theoretically, Tarkenton was supposed to throw his passes in less than five seconds, before his protection broke down and tacklers like Marchetti could get to him. However, the young and inexperienced Viking linemen were seldom able to hold off the pass rushers long enough to give Tarkenton a chance to pass successfully from within his protective "pocket." Minnesota had a bunch of "Watch Out" blockers, who often failed to stop the men they were assigned to block. When this happened they would turn around and yell at Tarkenton, "Watch out!"

So Tarkenton would run for his life, dodging, twisting, eluding tacklers, desperately looking down-field for a receiver. Sometimes he got the ball away, but sometimes he had to run the ball back to the line of scrimmage. Frequently the angry, frustrated

Before Tarkenton can throw the ball he is hit hard by Gino Marchetti (89).

linemen and backs, embarrassed by his frenzied scrambling, would tackle him all at once from behind, from the side, and from the front. Tarkenton refused to play the game according to tradition, so the defense often threw the book at him.

The crunching sound made by 500 pounds of well-muscled, onrushing tacklers as they hit the 6-foot 196-pound Tarkenton was a fearsome noise. Fans in the stands would scream and Minnesota coach Norm Van Brocklin would cringe on the sidelines. Then the officials would gingerly untangle the pile of tacklers to see if Fran had survived the play uninjured.

Invariably Tarkenton would jump up, clap his hands together and rush back to another huddle. In his own mind Tarkenton had accepted the necessity of such beatings and he knew he could take them. To applauding fans he seemed fearless.

"I'm not afraid of getting hit," he said. "The average fan has just as much courage as I do. When I see that those big guys will get me I just flop down and act like a wet dish rag. When I'm under a pile of pass rushers I just relax and plan my next play."

Despite Gino Marchetti's dire prediction, it soon became apparent that Fran Tarkenton would be around for many more plays and many more years of pro football.

"I expect to be playing when I'm thirty-nine," Tarkenton said. "There's no reason why I should lose my quickness. I may lose some speed, but being able to run fast is not essential for scrambling."

Tarkenton had been quick on his feet ever since his boyhood days. Fran had been born in Washington, D. C.; but his father, who was a Methodist minister, moved the family to Georgia in the early 1940s. In 1951 the Tarkentons moved to Athens, Georgia, where Fran joined the Little League program. He had been recruited by his seventh-grade teacher, Mrs. Whatley, whose husband coached Little League, in addition to being the baseball

Tarkenton hands off to halfback Tom Michel.

coach at the University of Georgia. Fran played shortstop and he also pitched, helping to lead his team to the Athens Little League championship in 1952.

Tarkenton enjoyed his Little League experience.

"We had good adult leadership, especially in Jim Whatley. He had a very strong influence on my life. In fact, he was one of the main reasons I went to the University of Georgia. And he's still a good friend."

Athens is the home of the University of Georgia, where football dominates campus life in the fall of the year. To the local youth the Georgia Bulldogs are heroes.

Francis Tarkenton's idol, however, was Sammy Baugh, the legendary passer of the Washington Redskins. Young Francis had a healthy interest in all sports, but he had a particular faith in his football abilities. By the time he was a sophomore at the University of Georgia, he was certain that he was the man to take charge of the Bulldogs and lead the team to a Southeastern Conference title. He was a third-string quarterback when the year began, but at season's end he was sharing the starting role. As a junior, Tarkenton played 80 percent of the time, was voted to the all-conference team and led Georgia to a 14–0 victory over Missouri in the Orange Bowl.

Although many people thought he would be selected as an All-America in his senior year, Tarkenton suffered a series of disappointments. The Bulldogs played poorly and, as a result, critics blamed the Georgia quarterback. In addition, injuries kept Fran out of the last two games of the season. And when the pros held their college draft Tarkenton was passed by until the third round.

Tarkenton had hoped to be Washington's number one choice, in spite of the fact that a Redskin scout had once told him that his arm was weak. Fran thought that the criticism was groundless.

"The ability to throw a ball seventy yards is the most overestimated talent a quarterback can have," he says. "The long pass is easy. It's the short ball that's hard to throw properly."

Tarkenton could have signed a contract for more money with the Boston Patriots of the American Football League, but he chose Minnesota and the NFL instead.

"I wanted those people who passed me up in the draft to eat crow," said Fran.

Professional linebackers relished the thought of facing a preacher's son named Francis. In their minds Tarkenton had to be too nice to survive in the violent world of pro football. It wasn't long before the Chicago Bears initiated Tarkenton as a pro quarterback.

"They put on the blitz all afternoon and I didn't have the slightest idea what to do about it," Tarkenton recalls. "I was massacred."

The Bears called their blitz "the crazy rush." While the opposing quarterback called signals the Bears would shout insults, promising to bury him in a pile of tacklers. And when the ball was snapped seven Bear players would charge the unfortunate quarterback.

"In college," Tarkenton said, "I'd drop back five yards and set up to pass. In the pros I had to learn to get back seven yards because at five they'd be all over me."

Beaten up by the Bears' blitz, Tarkenton nevertheless impressed Van Brocklin by passing for four touchdowns. The Vikings upset the Bears, 37–3. Van Brocklin nicknamed Fran "Peach" and expressed the hope that his education as a pro wouldn't take too long.

"Francis got up no matter how hard they belted him," said Van Brocklin. "But he had to learn that quarterbacks don't win by running the ball. They win by throwing it. That's what they get paid for."

Although Van Brocklin wanted him to pass more often, Tarkenton still had to run a great deal just to get a chance to throw his passes. And when his "scrambling" tactics were successful the crowds were delighted. Tarkenton refused to take a loss when a play proved unsuccessful. Still holding the ball, he would quickly move around the backfield, sometimes 30 and 40 yards behind the line of scrimmage, trying to find a way to go forward. He felt that looking bad and winning was better than looking good and losing.

Two weeks after the Bears' game, Tarkenton shocked Marchetti and the Colts by almost upsetting them in a close game. The Vikings lost, 33–34. Throughout the rest of the season, Fran scrambled and the Vikings fought doggedly on, learning a little from each game. They won three and lost eleven. It was not a bad record for an expansion team in its first season.

"I was lucky I wasn't killed," Tarkenton later recalled. "I knew so little and had so much to learn."

Rarely does a rookie quarterback ever get a starting job in the NFL. Usually it takes several years for him to mature. But the Vikings were a new team and Tarkenton was their only promising quarterback at the time. He *had* to grow up fast. Week after week Van Brocklin and his assistant coaches filled Fran's head full of vital information only to see him run out into the open during a game and risk serious injury.

"A quarterback has to love football," says Tarkenton. "He has to spend more time at it than any other player in order to perfect his abilities."

Fran's second season was tougher than the first. Minnesota won two, tied one and lost 11. Tarkenton threw 22 touchdown passes, but 5 of his passes were intercepted.

"In college all I had to remember was my pass

With one leg held by a Lion tackler, Tarkenton looks for a receiver.

pattern," he explains. "In the pros I had to learn the defense first before I could apply my offense."

When he dropped back to pass, he usually had only two seconds in which to analyze the tactics of the defense. His split-second recognition of defensive formations had to be instinctive.

In 1963 Minnesota won five games; and in 1964 they won eight. In four years Tarkenton had run with the ball 175 times, had thrown 77 touchdown passes, and had made the Vikings a title contender. Van Brocklin called him the life and heart of the team.

Married to a former majorette from the University of Georgia, Tarkenton made his off-season home in Atlanta, Georgia, where he worked for an advertising agency. His religious upbringing had stimulated his interest in the Fellowship of Christian Athletes, for whom he made speeches all over the South.

"If it's God's will," he once stated frankly, "I want to win an NFL championship and become a millionaire."

When the 1965 season opened, it seemed that Tarkenton might have a chance to obtain the first part of his wish. The Vikings were a strong, well-balanced club that year. Even the offensive line seemed capable of protecting Tarkenton so he wouldn't have to run as much. Although he was known for his scrambling style, Fran preferred to pass from a protective pocket of linemen.

"You scramble off a busted play," he explained. "You do it when you can't do anything else."

In spite of their high hopes, the Vikings got off to a bad start. In their opening game at Baltimore, they couldn't seem to do anything right. The Colts bombed them, 35–16. A week later Detroit beat them in the last 30 seconds of the game. Despite Tarkenton's consistently good passing, Minnesota wound up the season with a mediocre 7–7 record, finishing fifth instead of first.

In his sixth year with the Vikings, Tarkenton suddenly requested to be traded. He had become a top-flight quarterback, yet his team didn't seem able to win. He had been knocked cold twice while scrambling. The mental pressure of calling signals sometimes drove him into depression. Viking fans, who liked to think they too were quarterbacks, booed him whenever Minnesota lost.

Norm Van Brocklin was ready to quit, too. Then he and Tarkenton talked over their problems and decided they'd both try one more season. However, six weeks later Tarkenton changed his mind and renewed his request for a trade. The next day Van Brocklin retired.

The Fran Tarkenton era had ended in Minnesota. But the New York Giants were in desperate need of a good quarterback. And Giant coach Allie Sherman felt that Tarkenton's scrambling style would be an added advantage for New York. In 1966 Tarken-

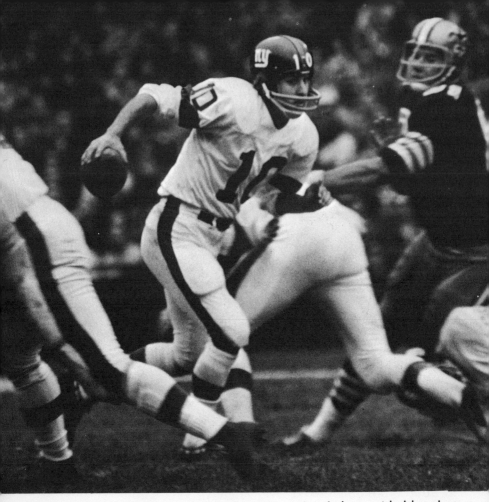

Tarkenton gains yardage through a hole provided by alert Giant blockers.

ton had run for 376 yards and four touchdowns, both figures surpassing the best of any Giant running back that season.

When Tarkenton joined New York, Giant fans saw in him new promise of leadership and excitement. Above everything else Tarkenton had faith in himself and in his goals as the Giant quarterback.

"I want my team to win a world's championship," he stated. "And I feel it can be done, I know it can be done. I believe in it."

If his new teammates show the same confidence, Fran Tarkenton may lead them to a world championship—without having to wait until he's 39 to do so.

5.
BILL BRADLEY
The Making of a Superstar

Modern college basketball has produced many outstanding players. But if the experts had to select two men as the best players of the years between 1956 and 1965, the most likely choices would be Oscar Robertson and Bill Bradley. Robertson was big and fast, naturally gifted and superbly coordinated. In contrast, Bradley was less impressive physically. And he had to become a star the hard way.

College coaches who have seen both Robertson and Bradley play find it difficult to choose between them. Each was a three-time All-America player. Each was expert at ball handling, playmaking, shooting, rebounding and guarding opponents on defense. And both were selected as College Player-of-the-Year in their senior seasons.

In 1960 Robertson led an excellent, well-balanced University of Cincinnati team to the NCAA championship, setting a one-game scoring record in the national tournament. In 1965 Bradley, playing with less talented teammates, drove Princeton to the nationals, too. Although Princeton lost in the semifinals, Bradley broke Robertson's scoring mark in the game that determined third place in the tournament. That contest, Bradley's final collegiate appearance, produced his finest effort and one of the greatest "one-man shows" in college-basketball history.

Until Bradley came along, Oscar Robertson had been considered the best college player of all time. He was in a class by himself. Even professional coaches were awed by Robertson's talent. Yet, when Red Auerbach first saw Bradley play at Princeton, he said that Bill was already in a class with "The Big O." At the time Auerbach was doing a brilliant job of coaching the Boston Celtics, the best team in pro basketball.

Other professional coaches were equally excited by Bradley's abilities. Coach Alex Hannum, whose Philadelphia 76ers eventually dethroned the Celtics, said:

"Bradley just seemed to know what to do, when to do it, and how to get it done."

The pro teams eagerly awaited the time when Bradley would be able to sign a professional contract. The New York Knickerbockers had had their eyes on him even in his sophomore year, and in 1963 they had reserved territorial draft rights to him. But the Knicks wouldn't be able to obtain his services until 1965, when he would be graduated from

Princeton. The big question in the minds of most basketball people was whether Bradley was really as good as Robertson. How would the performances of the two players compare in the National Basketball Association? Critical fans, as well as the Knickerbockers, were eager to find out. Then, on the eve of his graduation, Bradley announced that he would not turn pro. He explained that he was taking a Rhodes Scholarship in order to pursue his education at Oxford.

To Bradley, being a Rhodes Scholar was more important than playing basketball. To those fans who were disappointed because they would not see a meeting between him and Robertson, Bradley stated:

"Oscar Robertson is the best basketball player alive!"

That modest judgment satisfied no one, particularly those who knew Bradley well. They realized that if Robertson was the number-one player, then Bradley would have to settle for second best, and never in his life had Bradley been happy being anything but the best.

Bill Bradley was born in Crystal City, Missouri, the only child of wealthy parents. His father was president of the Crystal City State Bank. His mother was a former teacher who had played basketball in her high school days. Young Bill was devoted to sports. He played tennis, soccer and golf, and he was also a good swimmer. At football he so impressed the coach at Crystal City High that a position as starting end was reserved for him even before he left grade school.

"You can be the best end in the state," promised the coach. To which Bradley replied: "No, thanks. I'd rather play basketball."

In his Little League days Bradley dreamed of glory as a baseball star.

"I used to think," he said later, "that I couldn't live unless I played baseball, but I eventually gave that up."

Concerning his Little League experience Bradley once wrote:

"Probably the most important lessons I learned were to be a good loser and a graceful winner; to put 100 percent into every practice and game; to subordinate yourself to team effort; and to realize that all is not lost if victory doesn't come your way. For these attitudes and the many lasting friendships I am forever grateful."

Although he was encouraged to participate in all sports, Bradley nevertheless realized that there were other things in life besides playing games. In high school he was a straight-A student and a member of the National Honor Society, in addition to being the president of the Student Council. He had good health and a friendly nature, and he was popular among his schoolmates despite his family's wealth.

In basketball he found a sport in which he could help others to achieve success. As a playmaking ball handler he could coordinate his team's efforts. And as he perfected his own talent, he found that he served as a source of inspiration to his teammates.

Bradley practiced for perfection. His daily schedule on the basketball court was time-consuming, rigorous and effective. He practiced 30 hours a week during the school year, and three hours a day during the summer, drilling himself in the fundamentals: free throws, field goals, jump shots, hook shots, footwork, faking, passing and dribbling. He couldn't run as fast or jump as well as other players, but his self-discipline and concentration gave him the advantage of confidence. He knew why he made his moves at all times and, as a result, he could control not only the ball but the game itself.

"The fundamentals aren't hard," he said. "If you've played enough basketball you don't need to look at the ball when you're dribbling or passing."

During his high-school career Bradley scored 3,066 points. His reputation lured college recruiters from all over the country. But when Bill decided to enroll at Princeton, hopeful college basketball coaches were shocked. Ivy League basketball was considered more of a pastime than a major college sport. Bradley's chances of becoming a national superstar appeared to be dim. Characteristically,

Bradley chose Princeton not for its basketball team but for its advantages as an educational institution.

"I don't need basketball competition," Bradley explained. "I love the game. It's a part of me. But it's not an inseparable part. What it gives me is a relief from studying."

At Princeton Bradley discovered that whenever the basketball team played at home they had to dress in a locker room that had no lockers or water fountains. In contrast, his high-school teams had played in gymnasiums that were better equipped. A ball and a basket were all that Bradley needed to show his ability, however.

Fortunately, Princeton had a good young coach, named Bill Van Breda Kolff, who felt that he could build a team around Bradley's skill. Van Breda Kolff naturally believed that winning was the object of the game, but he also felt that winning with style was even more important. In Bradley the Princeton coach had the supreme stylist. Bradley practiced every move, every technique that would help him to improve his game. Merely having fun was not sufficient. To win for Princeton was a challenge, and Bradley faced it with his usual confidence.

As a freshman he set a school scoring record with 398 points. He also set an NCAA record by sinking 57 free throws in succession. A year later he sparked Princeton for the first of three straight Ivy League titles, averaging 27.3 points per game, the fifth best record in the country.

In a postseason tournament game against St. Joseph's College of Pennsylvania, Princeton nearly pulled the upset of the year. Bradley scored 40 points and held St. Joseph's ace scorer to a mere nine points. When Bradley finally fouled out, Princeton had a five-point lead, and lost by only one point. The St. Joseph's coach called Bradley's performance the best he had ever seen in college basketball.

Bradley's junior season coincided with the 1964 Olympic Games. His scoring feats (a total of 936 points) and sparkling floor play led to his selection as a member of the United States Olympic basketball team. Bradley was the only undergraduate on the United States five, a veteran team made up of the best amateur players in the country.

Although Bradley had been accustomed to playing forward, the Olympic coaches asked him to play guard. They thought he was too small, at 6 feet 5 inches, to be an effective forward. Bradley's style made him a natural as a playmaker. He dribbled well with either hand, was willing to pass the ball to other players and had an incredibly wide range of vision.

A test of Bradley's eyesight had revealed that he could scan at a glance almost 10 percent more area than the average good athlete. Teammates swore that Bradley could see out of the back of his head.

Although he was noted for his scoring, Bradley amazed the Olympic head coach, Hank Iba, with his defensive ability. Iba assigned him to guard the scoring ace of each team the United States faced. Against Russia, in the Olympic finals, Bradley had to guard Yuri Korneyev, an aggressive shooter who outweighed Bill by 40 pounds. The Russian scored only nine points as the United States won the championship, 73–59. Bradley earned both a gold medal and an award as his team's most valuable player.

When he returned to Princeton, Bradley threw himself into a furious routine of academic research and social work. More and more, basketball became a means of relaxation. When he wasn't playing or practicing, he was studying or giving talks to youth groups. Among his classmates Bradley's study habits were notorious. He seldom slept more than six hours a night. During one four-day period he got only eight hours' sleep because he had to write a history paper.

Princeton's basketball schedule often called for Saturday-night games, after which Bradley would take the long bus trip back to Princeton to snatch a few hours' rest before he met with his regular Sunday School classes. Like Fran Tarkenton, Bill was a member of the Fellowship of Christian Athletes, and frequently spoke to groups of young people.

After returning from the Olympic Games, Bradley had applied for a Rhodes Scholarship. Just before Christmas, 1964, he learned that he had been accepted. The academic prestige resulting from his Rhodes Scholarship actually increased his reputation on the basketball court. Fans admired him as much for his brains and ambition as they did his footwork and hook shot.

The New York Knickerbockers, of course, were disappointed by Bradley's decision to continue his schooling. They had secured the right to draft him, but now he would be unavailable for at least two years. The experts who were comparing Bradley with Oscar Robertson would also have to wait.

In the Holiday Tournament at Madison Square Garden, Bradley put on a magnificent show. Playing against Michigan, the number-one team in the country, Bradley was pitted against Cazzie Russell, the only college player who could match his ability. In that game Bradley earned his rating of superstar.

Princeton had been given no chance to win, but Bradley wouldn't accept the predictions. Spurring his team to its best performance of the year, he scored 41 points. He made baskets from nearly every spot on the floor, rebounded aggressively and guarded his man tightly. With 4 minutes and 37 seconds to go, Princeton led by 12 points. Then Bradley's tenacious defending caught up with him, and he fouled out. As he walked off the court more than 18,000 fans gave him a standing ovation. And while Bradley sat on the bench, Russell led Michigan from behind to win by two points.

During his senior year Bradley scored a total of 885 points, averaging 30 per game and scoring on 53 percent of his field goals and 88 percent of his free throws. Princeton won 23 games and lost only six. Four of the six games were lost by only one or two points apiece. For the first time in basketball history a Princeton team earned a place in the NCAA semifinals. Tired and undermanned, the Tigers lost in the semifinals.

Princeton's next game, played to determine third

Bill and Coach Van Breda Kolff clutch the net awarded to Bradley after he has scored 41 points to lead his team to the Eastern NCAA Regional championship.

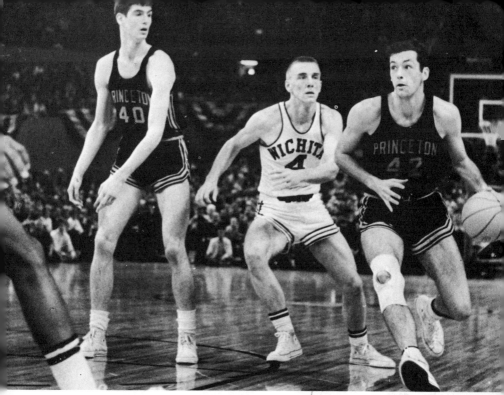

Bradley dribbles past Vernon Smith of Wichita.

place in the tournament, was Bradley's last collegiate contest, and it turned out to be his finest hour. The Tigers jumped to a half-time lead, with Bradley scoring 19 points. As the third quarter ended Bradley started to put on a one-man scoring performance. It looked as if he would break his personal mark of 51 points. As the crowd roared, Tiger teammates kept feeding him the ball, and he managed to sink nearly every shot. Without showing off, or even changing his facial expression, Bradley led Princeton to victory, scoring the last 16 points. He finished with a total of 58 points, breaking Oscar Robertson's tournament record by two points. With no dissenters Bradley was voted the most valuable player of the tournament.

When Bradley flew off to England for postgraduate study, there was grumbling among basketball fans. Some said Bill had turned his back on the ultimate competition against the best players in the game. They didn't care about his other ambitions in life; they wanted to see him play with the pros. How else could they tell if he really was as good as The Big O?

While Robertson steadily increased his already formidable reputation with the Cincinnati Royals, Bradley spent his off-hours playing amateur basketball all over Europe. For two years the New York

Bradley as a Rhodes Scholar.

Knickerbockers patiently waited, hoping Bradley
would come back and meet the challenge. There
were rumors that Bradley had no intention of playing pro basketball. Then, in the summer of 1967,
Bradley made another decision.

"One day in a gym at Oxford I was shooting
baskets. There's a thrill to driving in and making
a shot. I hadn't touched a ball for a month and
suddenly I got that feeling back again and I realized
I'd missed it."

The New York Knickerbockers were understand-
ably elated when they learned of Bradley's reso-
lution. They had a four-year contract worth a
half-million dollars waiting for his signature. They
told their fans that Bradley might be the one man
needed to make the Knickerbockers a contender for
the NBA title.

Typically, Bradley didn't make a big fuss over
signing his first professional contract. Organizing
his time to the minute, he took one day from his
studies and flew from England to New York. Then,
after only five hours' sleep, he got up at 4 A.M. to
work six hours on a paper he was writing about
Disraeli, a famous British statesman. At noon he
signed the contract that would make him the
highest-priced rookie in basketball history. Afterwards he held a press conference, ate a midafternoon
snack and caught a plane back to Oxford.

Circumstances forced Bradley to make his come-

Playing against the St. Louis Hawks, Bradley makes a jump shot in his first game as a professional.

back the hard way. Although he had obtained a deferment of his military duty in order to study at Oxford, he was still obligated to spend six months of active duty in the Air Force. The 1967-68 NBA season was nearly half over before he took his place on the court. At 24 Bill Bradley had been away from tough basketball competition for two-and-a-half years. He was painfully aware of the problems of regaining the top-flight physical condition and skills needed to compete with the pros.

"I expect to hurt," he said. "Real pain. The kind that is necessary for pleasure to be enjoyed. You have to suffer before you can succeed."

The prospect was a challenge that did not frighten Bradley.

"There never has been a great athlete," he has often said, "who did not know what pain is."

Experienced professionals also were eager to see how Bradley would perform. Most acknowledged his college achievements and tolerated his academic ambitions, but they were doubtful about his ability to measure up to the best basketball players in the business. As Ed Macaulay, an ex-pro star and an astute critic, put it prior to Bradley's debut with the Knicks:

"Until he plays as a pro we'll never know how good he is. And he won't either."

That's the kind of challenge a genuine superstar loves to meet.

6.
JOEY JAY
The Head of the Class

Joey Jay was an outstanding big league pitcher for 13 years. Yet he is most often remembered as the first Little Leaguer to play in the majors. However, Jay is not overjoyed by that distinction.

As a Little Leaguer, Jay was a big boy. His friends named him "Jumbo." When he was 12 he towered over teammates and opponents. On the Little League mound he intimidated batters with his size as well as his fast ball. Yet, in spite of his prowess, he was not the star of his team in Middletown, Connecticut.

"Our team went all the way to the 1948 Little League World Series in Williamsport," Jay once told a sports writer, "and our shortstop had his picture in *Life* magazine. By the time that boy entered high school he had lost all his interest in baseball."

As a result of his experiences, Jay has been less than enthusiastic about Little League. Although he himself went on to baseball fame and fortune, he feels that some boys are harmed rather than helped by Little League. Jay also thinks that occasionally the most fair-minded parents put too much pressure on their boys. "Even those who don't interfere in Little League find it difficult to conceal their disappointment when their sons have a bad day," he says.

Jay insists that a boy can play baseball only as well as *he* wishes. His parents can't make him better than he wants to be. Natural talent is vital to a ballplayer, but self-determination is the key that opens the door to the big leagues.

Joey Jay himself wasn't pushed into the big leagues. To him baseball was fun. He liked to pitch, even when pitching became hard work.

When he first turned professional he had little fun because he wasn't allowed to pitch regularly. As a "bonus baby" in 1953, he sat on the Milwaukee Braves' bench because at that time there was a major league rule that forbade teams to farm out high-priced bonus players. In his first two-and-a-half years in the big leagues, he appeared in only 30 games and pitched only 47 innings. When he finally got a chance to show his ability, he had wasted nearly three years of his career. During his long apprenticeship he pitched only two full games, but he won both.

Jay was finally sent to the minors to complete his pitching education. In 1957, at Wichita, Kansas, Joey won 17 games and fanned 199 batters. His performance convinced the Braves that he was ready for regular work in the National League.

"It took me from '53 until '58 before I knew I was a pitcher," says Jay, with a wry smile.

With Milwaukee in 1958, he contributed seven wins to the Braves' successful pennant drive.

"I learned an awful lot in my first real season at Milwaukee," says Jay. "More than in the five previous years I was around. A pitcher needs some professional experience to understand what veteran big leaguers are talking about. Just listening to Warren Spahn talk pitching was educational."

Playing on the same team with Spahn and Lew Burdette was both helpful and frustrating. Jay was only a part-time starter behind Spahn, Burdette and Bob Buhl.

Along with Juan Pizarro, Jay was traded to Cincinnati on December 15, 1960. Although the Reds had no way of knowing at the time, Jay would turn out to be a valuable Christmas present.

When the 1961 National League season opened, critics picked Cincinnati to finish sixth in the standings. In 1960 the Reds had ranked sixth, and the addition of Jay was not expected to improve the club significantly. In eight seasons with the Milwaukee organization, Jay had won only half of his games.

For Jay the 1961 season started disastrously. Although he pitched well, he lost his first three games. In all three the Reds had failed to score a

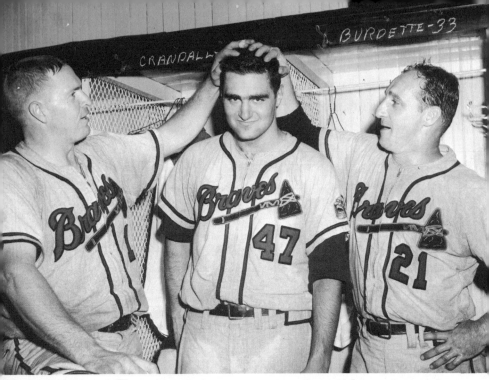

After hurling a one-hit shutout against the Cincinnati Reds, Jay poses with Milwaukee teammates Del Crandall (left) and Warren Spahn (right).

single run for him. May 1 had come and gone before Jay got his first victory.

Facing the weak-hitting Philadelphia Phillies, Joey thought he had a chance to pitch a shutout. If his teammates could score one run, he'd be happy. Fortunately, the Reds picked up two in the first inning and Jay was so overjoyed that he retired 24 of the first 25 batters he faced. The Phils threatened in the ninth, but Jay managed to avoid serious trouble and he fanned the final batter. Then he proceeded to do a little dance on the mound in celebration of his one-hit victory.

Having broken his streak of bad luck, Jay went on to win eight straight games. With Jay's help the Reds shocked the experts by driving into first place. Jay did not lose another game until June 20. But prior to that, Cincinnati had won six in a row, putting the Reds two games ahead of the rest of the league. Jay was having the best year of his career, and his performance was helping to inspire the club. On top of that, Jim O'Toole and Jim Maloney (another Little League graduate) were beginning to show the form that would make them big winners in future seasons.

But it was Joey Jay who anchored the pitching staff. He stopped the second-place Dodgers on a Sunday, then whipped the red-hot Braves four days later, knocking Warren Spahn out of the box by hitting a single in the fifth inning.

"Joey should get a bonus for his hitting," said a teammate.

Jay's selection as a member of the All-Star Team was nearly unanimous. A World Series victory was his next goal. With Milwaukee he had played in the Series, and he was excited by the prospect of competing in another.

August 15 was Jay's birthday, and on that date he won the opener of a vital three-game series with Los Angeles. The Reds went on to sweep the series, taking over the league lead for good.

Cincinnati had not had a 20-game winner in 14

seasons. As the pennant race went into the home stretch, it seemed almost certain that Jay would reach the magic mark.

On September 12 Jay went to the mound for his fifth start against Milwaukee. He had beaten the Braves three times, and as fate would have it, he was scheduled to pitch against his ex-roommate, Carl Willey.

In the fifth inning Jay scored a run, sliding bumpily over the plate as the throw from the outfield bounced away from the catcher. That was the only run of the game. Pitching slowly and deliberately, Jay blanked the Braves' slugging line-up. In the ninth he had to retire the heart of the Milwaukee batting order: Eddie Mathews, Hank Aaron and Joe Adcock. Each hit the ball hard, but it was to be Joey Jay's night, just as it had been his year. The Reds won, 1–0.

Jay picked up an additional win during the season, helping the Reds in their final drive for the pennant. Then, during the World Series, he pitched the only victory over the Yankees as Cincinnati went down in defeat. His 22 triumphs for the Reds during 1961 nearly matched his 5-year major league total with the Braves. The Little League bonus-baby had, indeed, grown up.

As the ace of the defending National League champions in 1962, Jay was a workhorse pitcher. He started 37 games, completed 16, and pitched a total of 273 innings. The Reds finished a disappointing third in the league standings, but Jay won 21 games.

Jay's second consecutive big year resulted in a substantial pay raise. His 1963 contract called for nearly as much salary as he had received in bonus money 10 years earlier.

"Baseball is a funny business," says Jay, "because kids who are barely out of Little League can get the same kind of money that's paid to established veterans!"

Little League officials in Middletown, Connecticut, were obviously pleased with Jay's big league records. They renamed their farm-club program after the star right-hander. Over 200 boys were soon learning baseball in the Joey Jay Little League.

During the 1963 season, however, Jay had more bad days than good. His critics were numerous and vocal as he struggled through the summer, winning 7 games and losing 18.

At the age of 28 Jay should have been at his physical peak. Because he was an established star, he was expected to attempt a comeback. And in 1964 Jay returned to form. He fanned four times as many batters as he walked, and he had the second lowest earned-run average of his career. His record of completed games was the best on the Reds' pitching staff.

Unfortunately for Jay, Cincinnati batters went into a rare "team slump" in 1964. Playing in the

| AT BAT 42 | BALL 0 | STRIKE 0 | OUT 1 |

	1	2	3	4	5	6	7	8	9	10	R	H	E	IG
CINCINNATI	3	0	0	0	0	0	0	0	0		3	7	0	4
N.Y.METS	0	0	0	0	1	0	0	0			1	5	1	1

as good
to your
taste

as it is
to your
thirst

Who says a

371

smallest park in the league, where opposing teams
could hit more homers, the Reds desperately needed
runs to win ball games. But base hits were a rarity.
Jay wound up with an even record—11 wins, 11

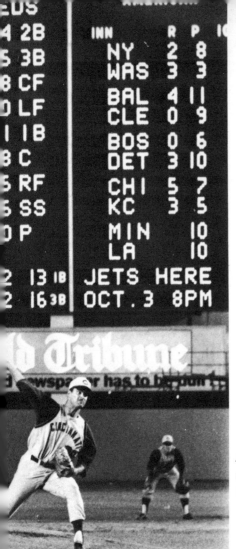

After being traded to Cincinnati, Jay pitches against the
New York Mets.

losses. It was the last season in which he was to win
more than 10 games.

In 1965 the Reds reversed the pattern of their
team performance. Their batting was terrific and

their pitching was poor. Jay, though he won nine and lost eight, completed only four of his 24 starts. His 4.21 earned-run average was the second worst of his big league career in (1963 his E.R.A. was .429).

Opponents said that Jay had lost his fast ball and the snap on his curve. Jay pitched a couple of three-hit games, one against the Dodgers in May, another against Houston in July. But for the first time in his career with Cincinnati he completed a season without pitching a shutout.

Joey ignored his critics. Ten years of experience had made him an "old head," who could pitch with cunning as well as speed. While attending the 1966 training camp at Tampa, Florida, Jay for once had a fine spring. He had always been a slow starter in the past, but when Opening Day came Jay was in midseason form.

Therefore it was a shock to Joey and a surprise to the rest of the league when the Reds traded him back to the Braves in early June. He was one of the five remaining members of the 1961 pennant champions. To be discarded in a minor trade was a rude jolt to Jay's pride.

After he was injured in his first start with Atlanta, Jay was of limited use to the Braves and they released him at the end of the season. He joined the Philadelphia Phils to start the 1967 season, but developed a sore arm. He agreed to go back to the minors to get into shape.

Once a week Jay commuted by plane from his home in Spencer, West Virginia, where he managed his oil business, to the Phils' Portsmouth, Virginia, farm club. But his unique part-time pitching plan didn't work out. Although Jay won three of his four games with Portsmouth, in midsummer the club released him. Jay insisted that he could still help some major league team, but it was the end of the road for Little League's most famous graduate.

Over four million boys have played baseball in Little League programs since Joey Jay pitched in the 1948 World Series at Williamsport. In 1967 more than 1,200 Little League graduates were playing in organized baseball. Eighty percent of the major leaguers of the future will probably have had some Little League experience.

They could have no better example than Joey Jay. He was one of the best.

7.
RON SANTO
Hard-Nosed Hustler

"When I signed with the Cubs they told me I was going to play third base. Now, one thing I knew about guys who played third. They were always getting their noses broken!"

Ron Santo has had his legs cut, his arms bruised and his jaw fractured. But, in seven years as the third baseman of the Chicago Cubs, he has never suffered a broken nose by fielding a ball.

"Maybe I'm just lucky!" says Santo.

Few baseball experts would call Santo's record lucky. He has been the best third baseman in the Cub's history. In 1966 he set a National League record for assists by a third baseman, spearing 391 ground balls and turning them into outs. His sprawling, lunging, quick-handed snatches of hard-hit balls are admired even by Brooks Robinson, the widely acclaimed Baltimore Orioles' third baseman. Yet Santo is modest about his fielding performances.

"If you dive at enough balls," he says, "you'd be surprised how many you come up with."

Baseball fans appreciate Santo's hustle on the field. And his aggressive attitude towards the game has earned him the respect of his fellow professionals.

"Every time you go on the field," says Santo, "you gotta push yourself. You can't give an inch. You can never let yourself get lax."

Because of his physical and mental toughness, Santo has often been called "hard-nosed." As he defines the term, "A hard-nosed player is determined to beat you any way he can. If he's not hitting he makes the big play in the field. If he misses a ball he makes up for it with his bat. Or he takes an extra base, breaks up a double play, steals home, anything to make up for his error. He tries to do everything he can to win."

Santo started his career in pro baseball as a batboy with the Seattle Rainiers, a club in the Pacific Coast League. "When I wasn't working at the ball park," Santo recalls, "I was playing for the Little League Italian Club. I was a shortstop and a pitcher. I learned a little bit and had a lot of fun."

Unlike Jay, Santo had a happy Little League experience. And, as a result, in 1966 he decided to sponsor his own Little League team in Park Ridge, Illinois, where he owns a pizzeria.

"So long as a kid's parents don't get too excited, he can learn a lot in Little League," says Ron. "He's gonna win some. He's gonna lose some. He's gotta get used to that. Everybody hates to lose, I know. We used to cry sometimes. Then we'd have a pizza, forget the game and get ready for the next one."

In high school Santo played football almost as well as baseball. In one football game for Franklin High, he gained nearly 500 yards with his passing. On the baseball team, he was a third baseman or a catcher. Playing in a city-wide all-star game, he hit a homer, drove in four runs, and threw out two runners trying to steal bases. After he finished high school, he received offers to turn professional from 10 major league clubs.

"I had worked up from batboy to clubhouse boy for Seattle," Santo says. "It was great working around the ball park. But when the Cubs offered me a bonus and a chance to play third base at San Antonio in the Texas League, I grabbed it."

In 1959, Santo played a full season at San Antonio. In 1960, he was shifted to Houston, but he played there only half a season before the Cubs called him to Chicago.

When Santo joined the Cubs, he was 20 years old and had been a professional for just one-and-a-half years. And, like most rookies, he had problems throwing, running the bases, and hitting to the opposite field. But he studied the techniques of good fielders, hitters and base-runners. Practicing constantly, he gradually gained control over his erratic arm, lost his clumsiness on the bases and became a consistent long-ball threat at the plate.

Santo admits, "I still had a lot to learn, but the Cubs gave me a good shot. By the end of the '61 season I thought I had proved myself."

His optimism was well-grounded. His batting average in 1961 was a healthy .284, and he had hit 23 homers and had batted in 83 runs. Fans, coaches, and even critics predicted he would get even better.

Unfortunately Santo got off to a bad start in 1962.

"I had had slumps before and got out of them," he recalls, "Everybody said to me, 'Don't worry, the cream will come to the top.'"

But Santo finished the season with only a .227 batting average, far below expectations. However, he did drive in 83 runs, equaling his total for the

Santo heads for first on a base hit.

year before; and he established himself as a superior defensive third baseman. He also learned a lesson:

"The cream doesn't come to the top automatically in baseball," he said. "You have to break a slump yourself. You have to work harder when things aren't going right."

In spring training, 1963, Santo worked extra hours to make sure he would be in midseason form by the opening day of the season. He had no genuine competition for his third base job, but he played as if he had. Daring anybody to take his position, Santo built up his reputation as a "hard-nose."

Bob Kennedy, the Cubs' veteran coach, once said about Santo: "Ron takes the whole world on his shoulders during a game. He thinks he's got to be perfect on the field and when he isn't the world's coming to an end!"

In 1963, Santo drove himself hard all season. Promoted to cleanup position in the batting order, he belted 25 homers, batted in 99 runs, and hit .297. Throughout the league, he became known as an excellent two-strike hitter.

"Actually, I'm a better hitter with two strikes on me than on any other pitch," says Santo. "I know I hit more homers after two strikes."

The ability of a player to bear down harder, to concentrate better when behind on the ball-strike count has always been considered the measure of a good hitter. Many batters hit best on the first pitch or when they are ahead of the pitcher. But if they are poor two-strike hitters they seldom earn a reputation for being "dangerous."

"I've had coaches and managers tell me that I let too many good pitches go by," says Santo, who likes to analyze his hitting technique. "It's true that I never used to make up my mind till after the first pitch went by. Then I'd relax."

Leo Durocher, who took over as Cub manager in 1966, has often loudly criticized Santo from the players' bench for letting the first pitch go by for a strike. Durocher wants his batters to be ready to swing at the first pitch, if it is a good one. But Santo is confident about his hitting. He knows that certain pitchers are in the habit of throwing him particular pitches, which he often hits for extra bases. He feels that he can afford to wait for those pitches.

Self-confidence is a basic part of Santo's nature. It has helped to make him a great fielder and a good base runner. In 1964 he became the hardest-hitting third baseman in Cub history. For the first time in his career, he hit 30 home runs. No Cub third baseman had ever hit as many. Santo also batted in 114 runs, hit .313 and was named to the National League All-Star team.

For 10 years Ernie Banks had been the acknowledged leader of the Cubs. Banks was still a dangerous hitter, but after 1964 Santo was recognized as the star who could inspire the other Cub players. As a result, he was appointed team captain.

"Ernie was still Mr. Cub," says Santo. "But Ern's such a nice guy he can't get on anybody. There's no way Ernie can kick guys in the can, make them put out a little bit extra. I can do it. Sometimes the captain has to do it."

Santo inspired his teammates with his bat as well as with words. In 1965 he hit 33 homers and batted in 101 runs. At the end of the season, to the surprise of no one, he announced that he had set minimum goals for the 1966 season. "I won't be satisfied unless I hit thirty out of the park and drive in a hundred," he said.

In 1966 Santo missed seven games after his jaw was fractured by a pitch thrown by Jack Fisher of the New York Mets. With his face full of wires, hardly able to open his mouth, Santo returned to the line-up two weeks earlier than expected. He reached his goal of 30 homers for the season, but he drove in only 94 runs. As a consolation, he could reflect on one midseason hot streak, when he batted safely in 28 consecutive games, another Cub record. That year, Chicago baseball writers voted him "Player of the Year." There was little competition for the honor.

As Coach Kennedy once put it:

"Santo's like all great ballplayers. You point him in the right direction and forget about him."

8.
RICH NYE
Mod-Style Moundsman

Leo Durocher's Chicago Cubs shocked baseball experts in 1967. In 1966 they had finished last. But the next year they jumped to third place. His losers had suddenly become winners. Whenever Durocher was asked to explain this transformation, he properly gave credit to his players.

Leo Durocher discusses his baseball players in language that is earthy and direct. Of Ron Santo, Leo has said: "A real hard nose!" Of Glenn Beckert, he has commented: "This kid would cut down his mother to break up a double play!"

Speaking of Rich Nye, his young southpaw pitcher, Durocher would smile shrewdly and say happily: "Ah, yes! There's money in the bank!"

Back in 1954, when the New York Giants won the World Championship, Leo Durocher was their manager. That same year Rich Nye pitched for a Little League team sponsored by the First Savings and Loan Bank of Walnut Creek, California.

"We wore uniforms with felt letters in black and

white," Nye recalls. "My brother and I played in the same league. It was fun, but I didn't take it seriously. So my brother would get mad at me!"

As a teen-ager Rich Nye was not particularly interested in sports. Although he was a winning pitcher in high school, his primary goal was a college degree. At the University of California at Berkeley, Nye played for an excellent ball club. College baseball in California is considered a major sport, almost the equal of football and basketball. The relatively mild climate permits an extensive baseball schedule, and there is keen competition among students trying to make the team.

Rich Nye's fast ball was better than average, but it was not sensational.

"I never could really 'hump up,'" he says with a grin. "In college I threw all kinds of pitches— sinkers, curves, knuckle balls. Everything but a slider. I never thought about pro ball particularly. Getting my degree was more important."

In a way Nye was typical of the bright, modern athlete. He took his studies seriously and played ball for fun.

"The Cubs picked my name in the eighteenth round of the college draft in 1966," says Nye. "So you can see I wasn't exactly a hot-shot prospect! Still, my eligibility was over in school and I thought I'd give pro ball a try. The Cubs gave me a small bonus, five thousand dollars. That seemed to sur-

prise some people, since I got to the big leagues
so fast."

Three months after he turned pro, Rich Nye was
pitching at Wrigley Field, the home of the Cubs.

"I hadn't set the world on fire in my first couple
of pro games," say Nye. "Even at Treasure Valley
in the Rookie League I could see the big difference
between pro and amateur ball. I gave up six runs
in my first game."

Despite this rough debut Nye was at Treasure
Valley only long enough to prove he was too good
for the lowest minor leagues. He won two games,
lost one and fanned 36 batters in 31 innings. The
Cubs promoted him to Lodi, in the California
League, where the competition was tougher.

"In my first game at Lodi I gave up five runs!"
says Nye. "I started wondering about how tough
things would be as I got higher."

Rich quickly convinced Lodi manager Ray Perry
that his next step would be into the majors. Nye
struck out 95 batters in nine games, winning five
and losing three.

Nye's remarkable control made him a stand-out
prospect. In 69 innings at Lodi, he gave up only 17
bases on balls. College training had given him the
poise and intelligence needed to work out his
pitching problems.

"Control to a young pitcher is usually a matter of
just avoiding walks," said Nye. "All you hear is,

'Make the batter hit the ball. Don't walk him.' And that's good advice. But sometimes when you're in trouble you get afraid of making a pitch too good and having the batter break up your game!"

Nye had to gain confidence in his ability to throw a good pitch, so he wouldn't get into the habit of throwing a strike when in trouble.

"There's only one way to learn to pitch to spots. Practice on the sidelines. Practice some more. Keep practicing."

For Nye the result of constant spot-pitching was exceptional control. In less than three months he became a pitcher, not just a "thrower."

"Ray Perry helped me another way. Psychologically. It's sometimes tough to stay in there when you're really under fire. He made me realize I had to stay on the mound and get 'em out. A manager shouldn't take you out of a game to save your pride. That's when you have to try to become a pitcher. You *have* to shoot for spots. You have to *think* about a pitch, not just throw the ball."

When the California League season ended, Perry recommended a major league tryout for Nye. Early in September Nye reported to Leo Durocher in Chicago. The Cubs were buried in the National League cellar, a fact that gave Nye an opportunity to demonstrate his skills.

"There's one thing Ray Perry told me that I'll always remember," says Nye. "He said it was harder

Nye is shown pitching for his ninth victory of the 1967 season.

to pitch in Lodi than it would be in Chicago!"

As Nye understood it, he could expect better support in the majors than in the minors. He was in for a rude surprise. The Cubs failed to score a run for him in his first two big league starts.

"I was disappointed in losing," says Nye. "But I knew I was lucky to be up there in the first place. I could see where Perry was right in one thing. The defense was so much better, on the infield and in the outfield. But it wasn't going to be so easy to learn about pitching."

Because he was a rookie pitcher, Nye was expected to rely completely on his catcher's signals. Which pitch to throw, and when to throw it was no longer Nye's decision alone.

"In the majors there's more pressure on both the pitcher and the catcher," Nye explains. "You don't dare experiment on the mound. In the minors you could find out what happens if you change up on a 3–2 count or try a curve with two balls and no strikes. You miss that experience if your catcher won't let you try it."

When the Cubs broke camp after their 1967 spring training it was obvious that Rich Nye would have to learn how to pitch the hard way—in the majors. Durocher made Nye his number-four starter. Six weeks later Rich was the number-two man on the staff because ace left-hander Ken Holtman had been called into the Army.

Nye soon learned to take charge on the mound.

"If I wanted to throw a certain pitch and Hundley [the Cub catcher] didn't want it I'd step back off the mound. I'd be hard-nosed about it."

Fortunately for Nye, Randy Hundley was little more than a rookie himself. He was a tough, competent catcher, but he was willing to see Nye's side of things so long as Rich bore down on the batters all the time.

"Randy makes you work," says Nye. "He gets on you, tells you you're lazy and that you're not bringing it!"

Surprisingly, when Nye was "bringing it"—that is, firing his fast ball well—he appeared to be just as quick as any left-hander in the league. Opposing players, coaches and managers voted him the best young left-hander of 1967.

Leo Durocher was both pleased and amazed at Nye's consistent pitching.

"The kid's been a pro only six months," said Durocher. "*Six months!* Kids today must be getting smarter faster!"

Nye had no illusions about the effect his bright mind might have had on his pitching.

"I wouldn't pretend to understand this business completely. Pitching is not a true science. If you do things right you can still have a wrong result. If you throw the wrong pitch you can sometimes get away with it.

"Some balls right down the middle get popped up. I know that. But I don't operate that way yet. I want the batter to think that I'm trying to make a good pitch every time. If he's looking for something else you might surprise him with a fat pitch."

Often, however, a good hitter can confuse a big league pitcher.

"Take Orlando Cepeda," says Nye. "He's hit low pitches that are six inches off the ground for base hits. Throw him the right pitch at the right time, though, and you'll strike him out.

"Or take Roberto Clemente. He murders our pitching. And everybody else's, too. So in one game I get him out four times. Leo asks me what I threw. And I have to admit that every pitch was right down the middle!"

At 23, Rich Nye probably seemed like a boy to Durocher, who was old enough to be Nye's grandfather. To reporters Nye looked younger than he sounded.

"I like to smoke a pipe when I'm reading or listening to music," says Nye. "But I don't smoke my pipe in public because I look too young. Besides, pipe smokers are supposed to be contented people, and I don't want anybody to think I'm contented with my life."

In his spare time, Nye indulges in many interests. His musical taste ranges from classical composers to popular folk and rock-and-roll groups. He likes to dance and has a passion for literature. Although he relishes the applause at the ball park, he envisions a quiet future as a college teacher.

"My brother leads a perfect life, teaching at the University of Wisconsin," Nye said during the summer of 1967, when Rich was the toast of Chicago. The Cubs were the darlings of the town's northside fans and young Nye had never seen anything quite like it.

"It seemed kind of weird, but wonderful, how they carried on when we got up to first place."

The Cubs were on the top of the league for only an hour and a half, or until St. Louis could win the second game of a double-header from the Mets and take over the top spot. A seven-game losing streak extinguished Cub hopes in the middle of July. Rich Nye had won nine games by then.

A sore arm hampered Nye's performance during the last half of the 1967 season. Durocher rested him for a week, but the inactivity rankled the young left-hander.

"My arm was hurting and maybe I shouldn't have even tried to pitch. But if you're being paid to work you can't sit out just because you don't feel right. If it's my turn I'm gonna go to the mound even if I can't break a pane of glass."

Nye's willingness to pitch despite pain helped him hurdle a major barrier to maturity as a big leaguer. The soreness in his arm was not critical.

So long as the Cub trainer agreed that pitching would not ruin his career, Nye went to the mound.

Unfortunately, Rich's stoic attitude didn't get much sympathetic support from Cub batters. In three consecutive games Nye pitched well enough to win, but he was taken out in the late innings with the game tied or with the Cubs trailing in the score. In early September Nye made his best effort of the season. For six innings he pitched a perfect game against Los Angeles. In the ninth inning, with two out, he was protecting a 1–0 lead when Lou Johnson hit a homer. Nye was taken out for a pinch hitter. And though the Cubs eventually won the game, Nye didn't receive credit for his work.

"If I had been a little more experienced I don't believe Johnson would have gotten that homer," Nye said in the locker room. "I threw him a good fast ball down around the knees, but he was looking for it. I should have started him off with a change up or a curve ball."

Shrugging off his bad luck, Nye took his regular turns on the mound until the Clubs clinched their third-place finish. His final record was: 205 innings pitched, 120 strikeouts, only 52 walks, 13 wins, 10 losses and a 3.20 earned-run average. These are achievements that would please any pro who had been in the business only a year and a half.

Nye was happy but not carried away with optimism. He viewed the future realistically.

"The reason why I was a winning pitcher was because I played on a winning team. I had very few outstanding games. And thirteen and ten isn't exactly an outstanding season."

But perceptive baseball people will keep their eyes on Rich Nye. As Leo Durocher put it:

"He's gonna be a good one."

9.
ROGER MARIS
The New King of Swat

During the 1961 American League season, Roger Maris hit 61 home runs for the New York Yankees and made baseball history. It was baseball's greatest slugging feat since 1927, when Babe Ruth hit 60 homers.

"I don't think I'd ever want to go through it again," says Maris.

Roger's reluctance is understandable. His record-breaking feat gained him little praise from the many baseball fans for whom Babe Ruth is a legend. By comparison Roger Maris was an upstart, a mere mortal who had never even batted .300 in the big leagues.

Naturally, Maris resented the criticism. At the same time, he was stubbornly sure of himself. During the 1961 season, when anyone asked how he felt about Ruth's record, he said:

"Records are made to be broken. If I can hit 61 I will."

Maris was just 26 years old when his great season

began. The year before, he had been voted the Most Valuable Player in the American League. In the eyes of many baseball experts, he was an even better ballplayer than Mickey Mantle, who was already on his way to becoming a legend.

However, some fans resented Roger's selection as MVP in 1960. Mantle had hit more homers (40 to Maris' 39). Mantle was the crowd-pleaser, the recognized star of the Yankees. Maris had never even had a big year with the Cleveland Indians or the Kansas City Athletics, the two teams with which he had played before joining New York in 1960.

Mantle was also the symbol of Yankee power. There were so many sluggers on the club—Yogi Berra, Elston Howard and others—that both fans and sports writers tended to think of Maris as just another long-ball hitter. Yet he was the Yankees' key man early in the 1960 season. In game after game, Maris consistently drove home the tying or winning runs. On August 6, he led the club with 35 homers. But on that day, he hurt a rib while breaking up a double play. As a result, he sat on the bench for 25 days. He returned to the line-up before his injury had completely healed because the Yankees' manager, Casey Stengel, needed his glove and arm in the outfield. His homer production fell off, but Maris led the league in runs batted in, a big contribution to the Yankees' successful bid for the pennant.

Maris makes a one-handed catch near the Yankee bull pen.

At the end of the 1960 season, sports writers who voted for the league's Most Valuable Player gave Maris three more points than they gave Mantle. Although many fans objected to their choice, Mantle himself agreed with the sports writers.

Roger Maris was born on September 10, 1934, in Hibbing, Minnesota. The Maris family moved from town to town during Roger's childhood, finally settling down in Fargo, North Dakota. During the long northern winters, Roger and his older brother spent much of their time ice skating.

"I played a lot of hockey," Maris recalls. "My brother had to drag me out to play baseball in the summer. He was bigger than me so I didn't argue with him. But it wasn't until we got to high school that I really liked baseball."

As a seventh grader in Fargo, Maris played baseball in a league organized according to the Little League pattern. He was 12 years old and small, but stocky. "Actually I preferred football. It was more fun," says Maris, who considers himself a Little League graduate. "Now, if my boy wants to play Little League today, I guess I'd let him. Though I hope he wouldn't be bothered by parents who want their kids to be big leaguers. I just want him to have fun."

The Maris brothers both went on to play American Legion baseball in Fargo. Roger was named the MVP in the 1952 state Legion tournament. Later, major league ball clubs competed with college football recruiters to obtain his future services. He had a choice of going to college on a football scholarship or becoming a professional baseball player.

"I didn't have the patience for studying," says Maris. "College was out. Pro baseball looked like a better bet."

One big league club, the Chicago Cubs, told Maris that he was too small to be a pro. But the Cleveland Indians had no such reservation and agreed to pay him a bonus of $15,000. In 1953

Maris batted .325 in Class C ball. In 1954 he hit .315 in Class B ball. Promotion to Class A, then to Class AAA followed. His progress was good, but he was no phenomenon, just a good prospect who had proved that he deserved a chance to play in the big leagues.

As Maris grew older, his muscular torso expanded and his batting stroke fell into a smooth groove.

"I learned to swing a bat a certain way," he has recalled. "I swung that way all the time. And when I was in good form I hit any type of pitch and any kind of pitcher. But when I was in bad form I couldn't hit anything at all."

Roger's easy batting style was deceptive. He didn't grunt or groan or lose his balance after his follow-through. But his unusually strong shoulders, fine bat-control, and good timing resulted in exceptional power.

"When I hit a ball right it would go 450 feet," he says. "That's usually enough, isn't it?"

As a rookie with Cleveland in 1957, Maris hit 14 homers. But his .235 batting average was more promising than impressive. In 1958 the Indians traded him to Kansas City. There he belted 28 homers and was considered the best player on a mediocre ball club. In 1959 an attack of appendicitis hampered him during the season, but his .273 batting average persuaded New York that he would make a good Yankee. And, the following season, Roger's performance as the year's Most Valuable Player justified the hopes of the Yankee management.

With the opening of the 1961 season, the Yankees were favored to win the American League pennant again. And to the delight of Ralph Houk, the club's new manager, Maris got off to a fast start, playing even better than he had the year before. In the first three weeks of June, Maris hit 15 home runs.

"I'll admit that I started thinking about Rudy York's record of eighteen homers in one month," says Maris. "I had a crack at it, but in the next seven games I didn't hit another homer. Still, I had

After hitting his 29th homer of the 1961 season, Maris receives the congratulations of Mickey Mantle (7).

twenty-seven and figured I might get forty-five for the season."

During his career, Maris had gained a reputation for slowing up in the last half of the season. Injuries and illnesses had often handicapped him in the past, as they were to hurt him in the future. But in 1961 nothing seemed to stop him. In mid-July Babe Ruth's record was in jeopardy. Not only from Maris, but also from Mickey Mantle, Roger's roommate when the Yankees were in New York.

In 1927 Ruth had hit 60 homers in the course of 154 games. Maris would play eight more games in 1961, the first year in which the new 162 game schedule was in effect. Responding to pressure from old-time fans, Baseball Commissioner Ford Frick announced that any batter who wanted to claim the Babe's crown would have to hit 61 homers within 154 games. The remaining eight games in the schedule wouldn't count for the record.

Maris soon felt the pressure from baseball fans, too. In mid-August, he whacked seven homers in six games, a new American League record. Stacks of letters piled up in Roger's mail box. Some correspondents blasted Maris, claiming that he was a terrible hitter, a poor excuse for Babe Ruth. Some fans wanted the record broken, but most of them wanted Mantle to do it!

Rogers Hornsby, a great hitter in his day who was already in baseball's Hall of Fame, said, "It would be a shame if Ruth's record got broken by a .270 hitter."

This remark was prompted by the fact that, although Maris was slugging as nobody had ever done before, his batting average seldom got as high as .280 during the 1961 season.

"Stengel wanted me to hit more up the middle," Maris recalls. "He thought I couldn't hit left-handed pitching and that hitting straight away would help. As a matter of fact, up until 1954 I was a 'ping' hitter. Then they changed me. I started going for the 'pump' all the time. Homers win more games than singles."

The Yankees, with Maris and Mantle pumping home runs out of every park, were winning the pennant in a runaway. As August ended, Maris had set another record by becoming the first man in baseball history to hit 50 homers by September 1.

"It was turning into a great year," says Maris, "but a miserable way to live. I couldn't go anywhere or do anything because of the crowds. They even asked for autographs in church. My hair started to fall out because of the strain on my nerves."

A 13-game winning streak clinched the pennant for New York in September. But the tension over the home-run record mounted. Mantle was no longer in the race, however. Because of a severe virus infection, he had dropped out with a total of 54 homers. He remained out of action for the rest of the season. Maris now had to endure the pressure alone.

With 151 games played, Roger needed only three more home runs to break Ruth's record. In Baltimore he hit one off Milt Pappas for number 59. Most of the opposing pitchers were giving him very few strikes at which to swing. Thus Roger went after bad balls, trying his best, but he wasn't able to hit number 60 until the Yankees returned home for the last five games of the season, well past the 154-game mark. It occurred during a game with the Orioles at Yankee Stadium on September 26. Oriole pitcher Jack Fisher threw his curve a little too high and Maris connected to send it into the upper right-field stands.

Afterwards, Roger said, "In a way I was glad I hadn't tied the Babe's record in 154 games. This was good enough for me."

Now, several thousand fans were anxious to see Roger hit number 61. A reward of $5,000 had been offered to the person who caught the ball that represented the record-breaking homer. On the last day of the season, the right-field stands at Yankee Stadium were jammed with treasure hunters. They booed Tracy Stallard, the Boston pitcher, when he gave Maris nothing to hit. With the count at two balls and no strikes, Stallard threw a fast ball into the strike zone. Maris swung—and connected.

"I knew it was gone when I hit it," said Maris.

"First time I ever won a 1–0 game with a homer."

Hitting 61 homers resulted in a great deal of personal and financial satisfaction for the new "King of Swat." But the shadow of Babe Ruth still hung over Maris. He repeatedly had to listen to critics who claimed he didn't deserve to be the best of all time. Fans demanded that he do it again by hitting 62 during the following season.

Maris hit "only" 33 homers in 1962, but he also had a total of 34 doubles and 100 R.B.I.'s. In only three seasons as a Yankee, he had slugged 133 homers and driven in 354 runs. Still, the fans weren't satisfied.

"Maris," said an avid supporter of the legend of Babe Ruth, "has proved only that he is an unsatisfactory hero."

Injuries plagued Maris in 1963. Two seasons later, he played in only 46 games. Bone chips in his wrist and strained ligaments in his knees had changed his batting style and slowed his base-running. Operations restored his health, but he was forever running into catchers' shin guards, outfield fences, and even other outfielders. From 1965 to 1966 he hit only 21 homers. In the fall of 1966 the Yankees finally traded him to St. Louis.

"Spring training with the Cardinals was wonderful," said Maris. "Nobody bothered me. I felt strong again. I had almost forgotten how much fun it is to be in baseball."

Maris hits number 61 to break Babe Ruth's record.

Cardinal manager Red Schoendienst gave Maris credit for the team's fast start in the pennant race. St. Louis had needed a strong hitter to fill the middle of the line-up. Batting third, in front of Orlando Cepeda and Tim McCarver, Maris helped the Cardinals to achieve a runaway victory in the battle for the National League flag.

"Even if Roger doesn't hit a lot of homers he does a good job," said Schoendienst. "He doesn't swing at bad balls and he hits the ball to all fields."

In the closely fought World Series Maris played a large part in St. Louis' victory over the Boston Red Sox, four games to three. Although Cepeda and McCarver slumped at bat, Roger picked just the right moments for his 10 base hits. His seven R.B.I.s set a Cardinal record for World Series competition. In two of his team's victories Maris drove in the winning run. In the fourth game he saved Bob Gibson's shutout with a shoestring catch. And during every game he ran the bases as if he was the youngest and not the oldest Cardinal regular.

Throughout the Series Maris suffered from a low-grade fever and had to take antibiotics every day. One shoulder was so sore that he had to take cortisone shots to relieve the pain. He confessed to reporters that he was thinking seriously about retiring when the season ended. The Cardinals hoped he would change his mind because, as Coach Dick Sisler said:

Maris is tagged out by Red Sox first baseman George Scott in a rundown during the fourth game of the 1967 World Series.

"Just having a pro like Roger around rubs off on the whole club."

One great season had failed to make Roger Maris the equal of Babe Ruth's legend. But then, Maris never said that he wanted to be placed on a pedestal.

"I never claimed I was another Babe Ruth," he said. "I was just Roger Maris, a guy trying to do the best he could."

A true professional, any way you remember him.

10.
DON SCHOLLANDER
The Machine

Teen-age athletes rarely earn permanent fame. Sports immortality usually comes only after years of basic training, hard competition, gradual maturity and repeated achievement.

Don Schollander was one of the rare exceptions. In the 1964 Olympic Games in Tokyo he won four gold medals. Don was then eighteen years old. Japanese sports writers who saw his feat in Tokyo's Olympic pool voted him "Swimmer of the Century." His achievement brought him instant election as a charter member of the International Swimming Hall of Fame.

To some spectators at the Olympics, Schollander seemed to set records every time he jumped into the pool. He established a new Olympic Games mark in the 100-meter freestyle race and a new world mark for the 400-meter swim. And as a member of the relay team he helped to set world records at 400 and 800 meters.

Most observers agreed that Schollander had done

just about all an eighteen-year-old could possibly expect to do.

Schollander's astonishing performance in the Olympics fulfilled a goal he set for himself on June 21, 1962.

"It snowed that day in Oregon," he says. "I had decided to move to California. My dad had convinced me that it was necessary to go there to get recognition as a swimmer. Since I was going to

Schollander swims to victory in the 400-meter freestyle race.

leave my home and my friends, I had to make it worthwhile. . . . I *had* to make the Olympic team and win that gold medal!"

Young Schollander's decision on that wet, cold summer day had a lasting influence on his life. To achieve his lofty ambition he had to follow an orderly, planned program. Don's willingness to channel his energies helped him mature faster than the average teen-ager.

"I had always enjoyed competition," Schollander recalls. "Right from the time I was a second baseman in Little League. The coaches we had on the Alpen Rose Dairy team in Portland, Oregon, made keen competition seem like a good time for all of us."

He goes on to say, "Besides teaching me lessons in winning and losing and providing me with lasting friendships, Little League gave me a tremendous amount of enjoyment, which, after all, is the main reason for playing baseball."

Schollander's talent for baseball was limited, however.

"The best thing I did was bunt!" he says. "What I liked best was that the coaches treated us to ice cream after the game. They made winning fun while they taught us some fundamentals. I learned that accomplishment is good for you. Competition makes you nervous, but everything in the world is competitive, so you've got to learn fast."

Don's swimming improved so quickly that at 15

he was competing in the national indoor championships. At 16 he tied the world record of two minutes
and four seconds in the 200-meter freestyle race. He
had gained national recognition two years before
competing in the 1964 Olympic Trials. His performance had also given him a reputation as a
perfectionist.

"Swimming," Don explains, "is different from any
other sport. There's no second chance. You have
to be ready to go in each race with everything
you've got."

In July, 1963, at Los Angeles, Schollander made
an all-out effort in the 200-meter race. His time
was 1 minute, 58.8 seconds! It was the first time in
history that anyone had swum that distance in less
than two minutes.

George Haines, Schollander's coach, said that
breaking the two-minute barrier in swimming was
a greater feat than breaking the four-minute barrier
in running the mile.

"Swimming is not a natural skill," explained
Haines. "It requires synchronization of lungs, arms
and legs. Don became almost flawless mechanically.
Other kids called him 'The Machine.'"

Under Haines' directions, Schollander perfected
an exceptionally strong kick and lengthened his arm
stroke. But his finest achievement was psychological.

"Don stood out," said Haines, "because he had the
will power to swim through 'the hurt.' That's the

point where most kids back off. They're afraid of how much it will hurt if they give that maximum effort."

Schollander explains that he masters the fear of overextending himself by thinking how good he will feel after getting past the initial pain.

In the 1963 AAU outdoor championships in Chicago, Schollander helped the Santa Clara Swim Club to set a world record of 8:7.6 for the 800-meter relay. That same month, while touring Japan with the Swim Club, Don lowered his own 200-meter record to 1:58.4. The Japanese swimmers, who were well known athletes themselves, compared Schollander to a hydroplane skimming over the water.

"I loved swimming in Japan," Schollander says today. "They idolize sports figures. After the Olympics I probably could have stayed there, endorsed Yamaha bikes and Sony radios, and grown old and rich!"

Schollander's record-breaking feats at 200 meters had virtually assured him of a place on the 1964 Olympic team. That summer he kept busy by breaking other records as well. At Bartlesville, Oklahoma, he smashed the American records for 200 and 500 yards. In a head-to-head contest at 400 meters with Olympic swimming champion Murray Rose, eighteen-year-old Schollander came into his own. Rose had won three gold medals in the 1956 Olympic Games. Eight years later he still held the record at 400 meters. But Schollander opened up a five-yard lead halfway through the race and Rose never came near him as Don hit the wall in 4:12.7.

That gave Don one world mark. The next day, Schollander set another record of 1:57.6 for 200 meters. And 24 hours later he tied the American record of 54 seconds for the 100-meter event.

"I had originally been a pure one-hundred-yard sprinter," says Schollander. "Coach Haines thought I had the endurance for middle distances, so that's where I concentrated. But when the Olympic Trials came up I had the strength to go both ways."

Don entered the 100-yard freestyle race in the Olympic Trials in New York City. He surprised himself by winning; and as a result he was qualified to enter five events at Tokyo.

Schollander's durability, which he thinks he inherited from his grandfather who lived to be 107, was unquestioned. His coach had an equal faith in Don's ability to pace himself for victory in any race.

"Don has a tremendous desire to win," said Haines, who was a coach on the Olympic swim team. "He is a thoroughly intelligent competitor with a wonderful tactical sense."

Schollander's reputation for setting records proved to be a help in forming victory plans for any race.

"I swim to win, not to set a record," he says. "If I win, that's the important thing. To win some races you may have to 'jam the pace,' that is, to swim

After winning the 100-meter freestyle event, Schollander accepts congratulations of Leonid Ilyichef of the Soviet Union.

slower. If you're a record-holder the other swimmers try to go as fast as you do. And sometimes they're afraid they won't get back alive! For example, if you swim the first few lengths in 59.5, they think they're swimming it in 58! They stay with you for a while, but then you pour it on and they give up."

Knowing exactly how fast to swim is the mark of a champion.

"I can tell just how fast I do each hundred yards," says Schollander. "I swim five miles a day in the summer, everything under the clock. I swim so many lengths that I get a sense of pace."

To some people, such hard work would be

drudgery. To Schollander it's fun.

"If it weren't fun I'd have quit in 1964. To compete at a high level of swimming you have to devote your life to it."

Schollander's four gold medals in the Olympics were honored as achievements of a lifetime. The Associated Press named him "Athlete of the Year." United Press International called him "Sportsman of the Year." He earned the Sullivan Award as the "Best Amateur Athlete" in the country. And in March of 1965 he received the Grand Award of Sports as "The World's Greatest Athlete."

Schollander displays his four gold medals.

"People want to know why I keep swimming," says Schollander, who is no longer a teen-ager but a member of the 1968 graduating class at Yale University. "I'm asked what else I want since I've accomplished just about all I can. When I was younger I wanted to prove to myself that I could win everything. And I did that. So my reasons for swimming are different now. Psychologically I still prepare for each race. But I think differently than I did at sixteen or eighteen."

Schollander could become the first American male since Johnny Weissmuller to dominate swimming in *two* Olympic Games. That's enough incentive to spur him on.

On August 1, 1967, Don swam in the finals of the Men's Long Course swimming championships at Oak Park, Illinois. There had been reports in the press that he was through as a top swimmer. Critics wondered if he was too old, at 21, to compete with strong young newcomers to swimming.

When the gun sounded for the 200-meter freestyle race, Schollander held the world record of 1:56.2, which he had set in a previous AAU meet. One minute, 55.7 seconds later Don hit the wall and was still the champion. He had set a new record, and his big smile reflected his new ambition.

"Most of America's top swimmers," he said, "stay on top about two years. I've been up since 1962. I'd like to see just how long I can stay there."

11.
JIM RYUN
Running Is Fun!

Like many great modern American athletes, Jim Ryun played baseball as a boy. When he was 10 years old in Wichita, Kansas, he had only a vague interest in the Olympic Games. And though he knew that Roger Bannister had been the first man to run a mile in less than four minutes, he had no notion of what that feat really meant.

"I wanted to be a big leaguer," Ryun recalls. "I played third base in the Sheriff's League [which is organized according to the Little League pattern] in Wichita. At least I played third until they found out I couldn't get the ball to first without bouncing it."

Although Ryun's arm was too weak for baseball, he thought that he might be able to compete in long-distance running. At Wichita East High School the skinny youngster went out for track. At first, his running was so undistinguished that he went unnoticed by Bob Timmons, the head track coach. In his first time trial for the mile Jim finished 13th, running the distance in a slow 5 minutes and 38 seconds.

He improved steadily, however, and soon Timmons was attracted by his raw talent. Ryun advanced from the B team to the top of Timmons' A team list. In his first state-wide competition, Jim's running helped East High to capture the state championship. The next season, in East High's invitational meet, he outran the state champion in the mile, setting a meet record of 4:26.4. Jim's time was over a full minute faster than the clocking for his first time trial.

Coach Timmons was so impressed by the improvement that he told Ryun:

"You could be the first high-school boy to break four minutes. But you'll have to plan. You'll have to work. You'll have to start thinking like a four-minute miler."

Ryun was tall, gangly and shy. He smiled constantly, but he spoke little. As a child he had nearly died from peritonitis. An ear infection had affected his hearing, and allergies plagued him. But when Coach Timmons told him to start thinking like a champion runner, Ryun accepted the challenge and went to work.

A typical Kansas schoolboy, Ryun had chores and studies to keep him busy. To his daily routine he added a grueling schedule of long-distance running. Every morning he would get up at five o'clock to deliver papers over a 12-block route. Then he would put on his running togs and jog six miles through the city streets. After school he would deliver the afternoon paper and then jog another six miles. Romping through rain, snow, and sleet, Ryun averaged 100 miles of running per week.

Distance runners rarely develop the necessary stamina for record-breaking races until they are in their mid-20's. Ryun had built up exceptional staying power and inner strength by the time he was in his midteens.

Coach Timmons outlined a rigorous program for his fledgling miler. Jim's daily morning and evening jogs were only one part of his training. He also had to endure workout sessions that included: a leisurely mile run to loosen up his muscles; four 110-yard sprints followed by four 60-yard sprints; a three-quarter-mile fast run; an 880-yard run; two 660-yard runs within four minutes; another 880-yard run; four 330-yard runs in three minutes; another 880; then six 100-yard dashes within two minutes and eight 60-yard dashes within one minute. Finally, Ryun would dash up and down a hill until he had covered a mile and a third.

Standing 6 feet 2 inches tall and weighing only 150 pounds, Ryun had the physique of a growing boy, but he gradually developed the dogged will of a determined champion. His friends and neighbors marveled at his dedication, but Ryun shrugged off the hard work.

"Thousands of athletes train just as hard as I do,"

Ryun with Coach Timmons in 1964.

he said, "and nobody remarks about them. If you don't train there are plenty of guys who will whip you in a race."

Ryun's original ambition was to make the track team and win his letter. Then a series of spectacular races assured him of not only a spot on the team but a place in high-school history.

In 1963, at 16, Ryun dominated the Missouri Valley AAU meet, running the mile in 4:08.2 and the half-mile race in 1:54.5. It was the fastest "double" ever run by a Kansas high-schooler.

Urged on by Coach Timmons, Ryun set his sights

on the United States Olympic Team and a possible gold medal at the 1964 Tokyo Games. Jim had always trained to run a "quality" mile, setting a fast pace from start to finish. But he had had little experience with "quality" competition, and the Olympic Trials were a revelation.

Ryun's only previous clash with some of the world's best milers had occurred in June of 1964, when he entered the Compton Relays in California. The Relays usually attracted a number of the finest competitors in American track. Ryun's mile was both scintillating and disappointing. Although he was knocked off the track halfway through the race, Jim's eighth-place time was 3:59. He had become the first teen-ager ever to run the mile in less than four minutes; yet seven men had outraced him.

Dyrol Burleson, the veteran miler who won that extraordinary race in which eight men had broken the four-minute barrier, was awestruck by Ryun's feat.

"There is simply no way to imagine how far Ryun will go after he becomes an adult."

At the early age of 17, Ryun had staked a claim to fame. He had also learned how rough it can be when milers of equal speed run in a pack. Ryun's response to this heightened competition was enthusiastic, though. From June until September he trained even harder for the chance to become a member of the United States Olympic Team.

The mile event in the Olympic Trials was held in the Los Angeles Coliseum. The first three finishers would qualify for the trip to Tokyo. At the starter's signal the six best runners in the United States leaped from their marks.

"I was in last place with only 150 yards to go," says Ryun. "I thought about all the work I'd put in and told myself to try harder."

Ryun sprinted to the tape, edging out Jim Grelle for third place behind Burleson and Tom O'Hara. Optimistically, Grelle had already bought his wife a round-trip ticket to Tokyo, hardly expecting to be displaced by a mere boy. But the Grelles stayed home and Ryun made the trip.

After Ryun arrived in Tokyo he caught a cold, which affected his overall physical condition. In his qualifying race Jim ran on the outside of the pack and placed fourth. His performance was just good enough to allow him to go on to the semifinals. In the next race he tried to run as if the gold medal was at stake, but it was no use. Weakened by his cold, he was in no shape to challenge nine tough, smart and experienced runners. Helplessly, he fell back from the pack until he was in last place, where he finished the race.

"After Tokyo," Ryun says, "I was ready to hang up my spikes. It seemed to me that every time I ran there was so much pressure on me to win. It had been more fun for me when I played Little

In the 1964 Olympic Trials Ryun edged out Jim Grelle (6) for third place.

League baseball and we won the Wichita city championship."

Back home from Tokyo Ryun nevertheless resumed his daily running. He had reached a climax in training for the Olympics and he had lost, but the depression quickly disappeared.

"Soon after a peak period there comes a new drive for another race," says Ryun.

Back with his Wichita East track team Ryun ran a mile in 3:58, another schoolboy record. After graduation in June, 1965, he took a full scholarship at Kansas University, where Coach Timmons had taken a job as head track coach.

At San Diego, in June of 1965, Ryun beat champion milers Peter Snell and Jim Grelle in 3:55.3, the fastest time ever recorded by an American miler.

Later that summer he traveled with the United States team to a dual meet with the Russians at Kiev. In that meet he took second place in the 1,500-meter race. Although he was internationally famous now, he trained just as hard as ever.

"It's hard work, sure," says Ryun. "Kids ask me if I don't miss a lot of life. Well, they've never been to Europe or Japan. I may not have all they have, but they don't have what I've gotten through running."

Two years after his first Compton Relays, Ryun ran again on that same California track. He won the mile in 3:53.7, a tenth of a second off the world record held by Michel Jazy of France. Six days later he broke Peter Snell's half-mile mark with a time of 1:44.9. It was only the seventh time that Ryun had run a half-mile race in competition.

Well ahead of the other runners, Ryun is clocked during the 1967 Big Eight Indoor Mile.

The Russians, in response to America's increasing role in the war in Vietnam, canceled a dual meet scheduled for July, 1966, at Berkeley, California. Meet officials hurriedly changed the name of the meet to the All-American Invitational. Ryun asked that the 1,500-meter race be switched to a mile race. The officials agreed, and on a sunny Sunday afternoon Ryun ran as only he could. Sprinting the last seven hundred yards, he demolished Jazy's world record, setting a new time of 3:51.3.

Ryun was no longer an awkward teen-ager. Just as he seldom stumbled in a race any more, he was no longer a shy or speechless boy. He maintained a B average as a freshman at the University of Kansas, and his camera hobby blossomed into a part-time job with the Topeka *Capitol-Journal*. He fulfilled assignments at such major sports events as the World Series and pro football's Super Bowl. One of Jim's photographs won a prize in photo-journalism, which thrilled him as much as a track victory.

"I guess I proved I could do something besides run," said the world's best runner with a grin.

Ryun had become the first American to hold the world's mile record since Glenn Cunningham, another Kansan, had run the distance in 4:06.7 in 1934. Jim was also the holder of the world record at a half-mile, and he held an American record at two miles. Within a year he was to set a new world's mark of 3:33.1 in the 1,500-meter run.

In February, 1967, Ryun won the Sullivan Award as the best amateur athlete in the country. His achievements had made him a recognized celebrity. Fans demanded his autograph and often tried to tear his clothes off at track meets.

"External circumstances can take away the satisfaction of winning," the young miler confessed in the fall of 1967. He was then in his fifth semester at the University of Kansas, enrolled in business school and planning his future. "I might retire from running simply because people expect so much every time I run."

Although he talked about quitting, Ryun still thought in terms of new goals and records. The gold medal that had eluded him in the 1964 Olympics might be attainable in the upcoming 1968 Games in Mexico City. Since that city is located on a plateau, 7,400 feet above sea level, Ryun would have to run in "thin" air. As a result, he would have to train himself to function on less oxygen than he was used to.

"A win in the Olympics would really knock me out!" said Ryun, referring to the high altitude. "So at Mexico City I'll concentrate on beating the best runners in the world instead of beating the clock."

In the 1967 National AAU Championships Ryun lowered his mile mark to 3:51.1. Physical maturity had added greater stamina to his sprint speed, and

In this race Ryun set a record of 3:33.1 for the 1,500-meter run. Here he starts to move past champion runner Kipchoge Keino on the final turn.

the prospect of running a 3:50 mile no longer seemed impossible. His body could accept it and his mind believed in it.

"It breaks down to running four 57.5 quarters," Ryun said. "That kind of pace can be discouraging when you think about it. I had never felt I could do it until this summer [1967]. Then in a race with Kipchoge Keino [a champion runner from Kenya, East Africa] I could feel the potential."

In the future new track records will surely be set by other runners. Meanwhile, as long as Jim Ryun continues to run, it seems safe to predict that the mile will get shorter and shorter.

12.
STEVE SPURRIER
Goldflinger

During the 1966 college football season, there were three outstanding teams—Notre Dame, Michigan State and Alabama. Each of them claimed the right to be called the number one team in college football. But oddly enough, none of them possessed a player worthy of the Heisman Trophy, the highest award a college player can receive. That honor went to a quarterback from the University of Florida— Steve Spurrier.

Even before the 1966 season started, Steven Orr Spurrier had been rated by the experts as the best prospect in college football. Professional football scouts had followed him for two years. The sum of their extraordinarily enthusiastic reports was that he had the arm of Sammy Baugh, the poise of Johnny Unitas, the leadership ability of Norm Van Brocklin and the quickness of Joe Namath. On the campus of Florida University, in Gainesville, the students called Spurrier "Goldflinger," because his passes were like money in the bank to the football team.

Spurrier's wealth of natural talent made him an idol to the football fans of Florida. He could get a standing ovation from the crowd by just walking onto the field. His feats on Saturday became legends by Monday. At the age of 21, he was sitting on top of his own particular world.

"College football is the best of all sports," said Spurrier. "And the Southeastern Conference plays the best college football in the country."

Fans from the Midwest, the Southwest and the Far West might object to Spurrier's regional claims. But, as a matter of fact, the Southeastern Conference was known for its fiery brand of football; and Steve Spurrier had contributed a great deal to the fireworks at Florida's games.

During his college career, Spurrier played 30 games for the Florida Gators. On eight occasions, when his team seemed hopelessly behind as they entered the final quarter, Spurrier sparked the Gators to an unexpected victory. His initials, S. O. S., were stamped on banners and shouted from the stands. More often than not, when the Gators were in trouble, Spurrier came to the rescue.

At the close of his final season, the Florida state legislature gave Spurrier an award for meritorious achievement. It was the first time an athlete had been so honored. In his acceptance speech, Spurrier

Spurrier passes against Missouri.

said that the most important product of his recent
national acclaim would be his ability to become a
positive influence on the youth of Florida. As an
active member of the Fellowship of Christian Athletes, which is made up mostly of sports stars, he
felt that his prestige would put him in a position
to promote the Fellowship's aims of sportsmanship
and fair play, on and off the field.

When Steven Spurrier was seven years old, he got
his start in sports by joining Little League. "I was
living in Athens, Tennessee," he says. "This boy
who played on the Little League team left town. I
got his uniform, and they let me play a couple of
games."

Although he joined the team by default, Steve
played Little League baseball for the next five years.
He recalls that, throughout his adolescence, he was
much more accomplished at baseball than he was
at football, right up into his high-school years. His
high-school football coach in Johnson City, Ten-
nesse, remembers that when Steve first went out for
the team he was "slow and awkward." However,
in his junior and senior years at Johnson City
High, Steve suddenly developed into a sturdy and
coordinated young man.

"I really grew a lot. Put on weight. It's true I
didn't set any records for the 100-yard dash. But
I had quick feet. I could move fast in the backfield."

As a senior, Spurrier made All-State in baseball, basketball and football. *Coach & Athlete,* a nationally distributed sports magazine, named Spurrier to its All-America high-school team. Following that honor, Steve received offers from many college football coaches.

"I wanted to play in the Southeast Conference," says Spurrier. "Since I was a T-formation quarterback I didn't see any future at the University of Tennessee. They still had the single-wing offense then. Ray Graves, the coach at Florida, was from Knoxville. He came to see me. I liked him. I knew Florida had a good climate. He convinced me it was a good place to throw a football!"

Ray Graves had been hired to make the Florida football team a championship contender. Before his arrival, the university had been known only for its high academic standards, and had placed little emphasis on developing its gridiron teams. Graves soon made Florida football lively. Steve Spurrier made it sensational.

There have been many fine quarterbacks in the history of the Southeast Conference—Charley Conerley, at Mississippi; Babe Parilli, at Kentucky; Fran Tarkenton, at Georgia; Joe Namath at Alabama. They were outstanding players, but Steve Spurrier broke every one of their passing records.

Although Spurrier was acknowledged by pro scouts as the best quarterback in college football, his reputation was certainly not based on his appearance. He was bowlegged. He slouched when he walked. And his teammates said he was always falling asleep at practice.

From the first game of the 1966 season, Florida was seen as a contender in the Southeastern Conference. The Gators were not as strong and well-balanced as some of Coach Graves' past teams. But Graves felt that he could build a successful team around his amazing quarterback.

"Old Orr is too much," said a member of the Florida coaching staff after looking at game films.

The Gators won their first seven games of the season. In one key contest, against Auburn, Spurrier booted a field goal with only two minutes and twelve seconds remaining, enabling Florida to win, 30–27.

"Kicked it from the forty," he says. "Ball was right on the hash mark."

Spurrier's fourth-quarter heroics were often breath-taking. Jokingly, sports announcers cautioned Florida fans with heart problems to stay calm or else stay home.

Although Spurrier was a superior player, he was not unbeatable. Georgia University's Bulldogs found a sure way to hold him down. In the fourth quarter of the Florida–Georgia game, the Bulldogs simply maintained complete control of the ball in order to prevent Spurrier from passing.

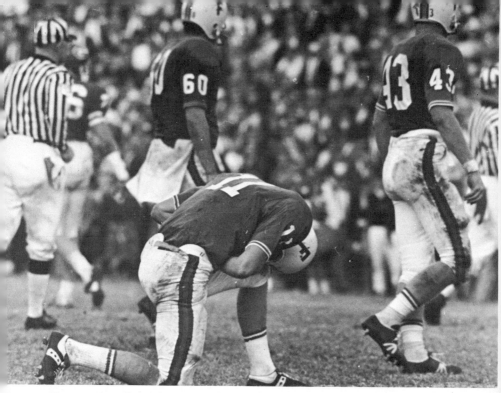

Spurrier kneels in disappointment after failing in his last attempt to pass against Georgia.

"They had us well scouted," said Spurrier after the game. Two of his passes in the last half had been intercepted. "That killed us," he said.

The loss to Georgia cost Florida a chance at the Southeastern Conference title. Then, later in the season, Miami University beat the Gators for the mythical state championship of Florida.

In spite of his team's losses, however, Spurrier earned the Heisman Trophy. He had completed 61 percent of his passes (179 completions out of 291 attempts), had gained 2,012 yards and had thrown 16 touchdown passes. Along with kicking off and booting field goals, he had also punted for an average of 40.8 yards.

His statistics were impressive. But Spurrier's coaches praised him even more for his ability to direct the team on the field.

"Actually," said Spurrier, "I'm a quiet leader. When I do well the rest of the players follow me."

After the Heisman Trophy ceremonies were over, Spurrier still faced his toughest test as a college quarterback. On August 11, 1967, he had to take the College All-Star team onto the field to face the world-champion Green Bay Packers.

"If we play almost-perfect ball we'll win," said Spurrier the night before the game. "We've got a lot of good material on our team. And the pros are not that much different. They don't hit any harder than guys do in college."

The Packers quickly showed Spurrier the error of his thinking. It was obvious that he and the rest of the All-Stars had a lot to learn. For example, how should an opposing team handle Willie Davis? That question had been bothering many fine professional quarterbacks for years. Twice Davis reached Spurrier in the All-Star backfield, causing him to fumble and lose the ball.

The Packers walloped the All-Stars, and the collegians were booed by the crowd. But, in spite of Green Bay's painful lesson, Steve Spurrier had reason to smile. The San Francisco 49ers were

Spurrier punts for the San Francisco 49ers.

going to pay him well to prove that he belonged with the pros. He had another chance coming, another incentive. Until then he had the memories of his former achievements. In college he had been the best.

13.
BILL FREEHAN
Iron Man with a Golden Glove

To field a baseball team a manager must find some player who is willing to catch. It isn't always easy. Good catchers are rare finds. The best are idolized by fans, by their own teammates, and even by catchers on opposing teams.

To be a catcher takes brawn and brains. Some critics say it takes much more brawn than brains. If a catcher was smart he'd be playing another position. The mask, shin guards and chest protector are a fool's tools, they say.

A catcher takes more risks than other players, and he sees more action, too. His throwing hand may be bruised by foul tips and wild pitches. His knees may ache as a result of bobbing up and down from his crouch while wearing heavy protective equipment. Base runners may collide with him on close plays at home plate, and managers and fans may disagree with his signals. Catching is a rugged and demanding assignment which doesn't look inviting to most observers.

"I never intended to be a catcher," says Bill

Freehan of the Detroit Tigers. He is one of the biggest, toughest and smartest catchers in the business. And he is frank and honest about his motives for taking the job.

"Back in Little League," says Freehan, "I was a shortstop. One day, a kid didn't show up and I was asked to catch. The coach was a cop so I did what he said."

Freehan played well enough to make the Little League All-Star team in Royal Oak, Michigan. During his four years with the team sponsored by the Royal Oak Tool Company, Freehan and his teammates won three league championships. Catching was fun, and it was also the best position from which to see everything that went on in the game.

"If I had a boy he would play in Little League just as I did," says Freehan. "I know I learned more about baseball than most kids my age."

One thing Freehan learned from his sandlot experience was that the pitcher often has an easier job than the catcher. In high school he worked on the mound whenever he could get someone else to catch. This experience probably helped him to understand what makes pitchers tick. Freehan's ability to handle pitchers is considered his greatest asset as a big league catcher.

"The biggest kick I get," says Freehan, "is to go out to the mound during a game and straighten out a guy who is having trouble. If I can do it, then I'm more valuable to the team than if I hit four for five."

Freehan has brawn as well as brains. In high school he was just as good a football player as he was a pitcher-catcher. The University of Michigan granted him scholarships in both sports, and he played both offensive and defensive end for "Bump" Elliot's Wolverines in 1960.

"I liked football about as well as baseball," Freehan recalls. "But the major leagues were expanding at that time. Catchers were in demand. As a sophomore I had led the Big Ten in batting. I was offered a lot of money to turn pro and I figured I might never get a chance like that again. So I signed up to play."

Freehan left college before graduation to join the Tigers for a reported bonus of $100,000. (Later, he went back during off seasons to obtain his Bachelor of Arts degree in history.) It was not a record sum of money, but it was enough to make many Little Leaguers think twice before turning down chances to become catchers.

Freehan quickly proved that he was worth his big bonus. After only half a season of minor league experience he was recalled by the Tigers. In 10 times at bat he belted four base hits. In 1962 he was sent to Denver, and against Triple-A pitching he hit .283 and drove in 58 runs.

"When I came up to Detroit to stay in 1963," says Freehan, "we had veteran pitchers like Frank Lary,

Freehan tags Rick Monday of Kansas City.

Jim Bunning, Don Mossi. They were old heads and knew what they wanted. I felt at times that they wanted an older catcher working with them— perhaps Gus Triandos or Mike Roarke. Sometimes I had to play first base instead of catch. But I learned a lot from those pitchers."

Freehan's rookie season was largely a success. Although he batted only 300 times and had to play 19 games at first base, his willingness to learn and to wait his turn as catcher impressed his managers, Bob Scheffing and Bob Swift. Both were former catchers themselves.

"It takes time to become a big league catcher,"

Freehan admits. "You have to get to know your pitchers. You have to get to know the hitters on every other team in the league, too. And you must have confidence and believe in adapting yourself to your pitcher's strength."

Calling the right pitch at the right time requires courage, as well as knowledge. Often a pitcher is afraid to throw the pitch that both he and his catcher know is the right one. It's up to the catcher to convince him that he can do it.

"When a pitcher doesn't have his good curve on a given day," says Freehan, "I gotta go out and talk him into forgetting his curve and trying his other stuff. With some guys that can be a problem."

In 1964 Freehan took over the job as first-string catcher. From opening day until the end of the season he was the spark plug of a Tiger team that made an exciting run for the American League pennant. Bill belted 18 home runs and batted an even .300. It was the first time any Tiger catcher had hit that well since the heyday of Mickey Cochrane, who had played for Detroit during the 1930s and was later elected to the Hall of Fame.

"Charlie Dressen was our manager at the time and he helped me a lot. I have to give him credit for polishing my thinking," says Freehan. "I must have spent more time in his office talking baseball than I did on the field playing. For a while Charlie called the pitches. I'd look over to the bench to see what he wanted before I gave the signal to the pitcher. But then Charlie lost a couple of games, so I took over on my own."

In 1964 Freehan's performance at bat overshadowed his excellent work behind the plate. There were no longer any doubts about his proper position. He still had his first baseman's glove, but it saw little action.

In 1965 Freehan set a Detroit fielding record. His .996 mark helped him to earn the Golden Glove award as the best catcher in the American League. On June 15, 1965, he tied a major league record by making 19 putouts in one game. Although his batting average fell to .234, he was one of few players on the Tiger roster who was marked, "Not For Trade."

However, by the time the 1967 spring-training season came around, Freehan was having some doubts about himself. He was widely acclaimed as the best receiver in the major leagues, but he was embarrassed about his hitting. For two seasons in a row he had batted .234, and his total of 22 homers was only four more than he had hit as a rookie in 1964.

"I've always thought I should hit twenty, thirty homers a year," he said. "The Lord gave me more ability with the bat than I've shown in the last couple of years."

Fortunately, the Tigers had hired Wally Moses

as their new batting coach. Moses was a highly regarded student of batting, whose theories and instruction had formerly helped hitters at Cincinnati and New York.

"Freehan's bat was a little lazy in the spring," said Moses. "So we moved him up toward the plate about half a foot. We had to make him attack the ball more. We made him want to pull more instead of hitting straight away. His front arm was dead. He wasn't popping the bat. But by the time the season opened he knew what he had to do and his bat was quick."

Freehan's quick bat got the Tigers off to a fast start. In Bill's first 33 times at bat he slammed four home runs and batted in 13 runs. Five of his hits produced the winning or tying runs for Detroit.

"Moses kept after me every day," says Freehan. "He'd stand behind the batting cage and remind me of the things I did wrong. Sometimes my arm would be locked when I swung the bat. I'd stride into the plate too much and I couldn't get the bat out in front. So I'd open up my stance a little bit."

Moses demanded that Freehan keep his back foot firmly planted in order to keep himself from lunging into the ball. Bill "planted" himself so solidly in the batter's box that be became an unmoveable target for "brush-back" pitches. Freehan found that the harder he hit opposing pitching the more often he would be hit on the left arm by inside fast balls.

In his first 50 games that season Freehan was nicked by 11 pitched balls.

"I never could move too fast in the box," Freehan ruefully admitted. "The year I batted .300 I was hit a lot, too."

Bill's body bruises multiplied rapidly. He was in the line-up day after day, game after game. Since Detroit's second-line catching was mediocre, Tiger pitchers wanted Freehan behind the plate where he could help them out. Freehan was willing to work, even though an occasional rest might have helped his hitting.

"Bill would hit .300 if he didn't have to catch every game," said Moses at the time. "Sometimes he's too tired to swing the bat!"

"I was hitting with more power than I was during 1964," said Freehan, "but even so, the homers were coming in streaks. I'd get in a rut for five or six games in a row and I couldn't figure out what I was doing. It helps to have a coach who can see the things you do right and remind you when you do them wrong in a game. But you still have to correct the faults yourself."

When working with his pitchers, Freehan reflected the same philosophy of "self-help." He might run out to the mound to remind his pitcher of the best way to get out of trouble, but there was only one man who could do the job—the pitcher himself.

"Belief in himself is the one quality necessary to a pitcher," says Freehan. "He has to have confidence in the pitch he's going to throw and know where he's going to throw it."

Whenever they work in Tiger Stadium, Detroit pitchers have a built-in handicap. The park is small and batted balls seem to jump into the stands for home runs. It is customary for pitchers to blame their catchers for calling the pitches that opponents hit out of the park. In 1967 Tiger pitchers gave up over 150 home runs, a statistic that Freehan and his staff remember with embarrassment.

However, no one seriously blamed Freehan for

Freehan slides home safely as the opposing catcher loses the ball.

the Tigers' pitching performance. Tiger fans and opponents heaped laurels on Freehan all season long. A total of 35 Detroit fan clubs, with 3,500 members in all, voted Bill "King Tiger of 1967." American League players voted him to the All-Star team, and he caught the entire 15-inning All-Star Game, which was won by the National League, 2–1. The manager of the Chicago White Sox, Eddie Stanky, praised Freehan as the most valuable player in the league. Freehan modestly commented:

"It's nice to have good things said about me, but Al Kaline is still the most valuable player on our club."

With Kaline and Freehan leading the way, Detroit battled Boston, Chicago and Minnesota until the end of the season. It was the tightest American League pennant race in years, but Detroit had a reputation for "down-to-the-wire" finishes. The Tigers' history included six championships. They had won the pennant on the final day of the season in 1908 and on the last weekend in 1940. And in 1945 they had won on the final day again, after losing on the final day in 1944.

On the last weekend of 1967 Detroit had a chance to take the pennant by sweeping a four-game series from the California Angels. Freehan caught all four games in back-to-back double-headers. Up to that point he had appeared in 155 games, a staggering total for modern-day catchers. Dead tired, his muscles sagging, he couldn't keep his pitchers out of trouble as the Angels battered Detroit into submission.

Winning two of those final four games gave Detroit a tie for second place. Bill Freehan had made the comeback of the year with his bat, finishing the season with 20 home runs, 73 runs batted in and a .283 batting average. At the age of 27 he was young enough to look to the future. Optimistic Tiger fans expected him to make their pitchers as good as their catcher. As Detroit pitching coach Johnny Sain put it:

"Our pitchers have an ace in the hole."

14.
TOMMY JOHN
Mathematician on the Mound

In August, 1967, the Chicago White Sox were in the middle of a tight pennant race, and pitcher Tommy John was an awful sight. He looked as if he had tuberculosis. His cheeks were pale and drawn. His uniform shirt-sleeves flapped loosely on his arms. When he ran across the outfield he looked like an exhausted marathon runner heading down the home stretch.

"I caught some kind of bug in the Army," explained John. "Got me right in the gut!"

The virus that struck Tommy John may have cost the White Sox the 1967 pennant. As the number-three man on a pitching staff that included Joel "No-Hit" Horlen and ace left-hander Gary Peters, John was frequently Chicago's most effective pitcher. When he pitched well he was excellent; and when he pitched poorly he was still fairly good.

"The way I figure it," said John, who was a math student at Indiana State University during the off season, "I'll just have to pitch shutouts to win this season!"

John's experience with White Sox hitting that summer brought a wan smile to his face one Sunday afternoon in September. The Detroit Tigers were at White Sox Park to challenge the Chicago club. Standing behind the batting cage, watching the Tigers take batting practice, Tommy sighed and said:

"I wish our guys would just swing the bat the way Detroit does."

Every member of the White Sox pitching staff had good reason to question the "hitless wonders" on his team. Pitchers get a feeling of security and

The weak-hitting White Sox were fortunate in having a strong pitching staff. Left to right are: Jim O'Toole, Bruce Howard, Joel Horlen, Tommy John, Gary Peters and pitching coach Marv Grissom.

confidence from watching their teammates score
runs for them. But the Sox seldom scored runs.
Their weakness at bat took most of the fun out of
pitching.

However, it cannot be said that Tommy John was
unhappy with the Sox or discouraged by his pros-
pects. Although he was still young, he had matured
rapidly as a big league pitcher. He knew the score.
If it took a shutout to win he'd make an all-out effort
to get it.

"If you know you have to pitch a shutout to win,"
says John, "you become determined not to make any
mistakes on the mound. You find out just how good
a pitcher you really are."

A good pitcher doesn't necessarily have a winning
record, as Tommy John learned in 1967. During one
stretch of eight games, Tommy pitched five shutouts.
Then, while he was serving two weeks with the
National Guard in the middle of the summer, a virus
sapped his strength. At the end of the season his
record read: 10 wins, 13 losses.

"Chalk it up as one of those years," says John.
"Things are bound to get better. I've already seen
the worst!"

For Tommy John, pitching has been a life-long
educational experience. Tall and slim as a youngster, John was not blessed by nature with a great
fast ball or an exceptional curve. But, after a great

deal of hard work, he developed a smooth delivery and a sinking fast ball. He learned the proper snap for a curve ball and understood the importance of good control. Adapting his talent to the fundamentals of the pitcher's craft, he made himself a competent professional. His success should be an inspiration to ambitious ballplayers of only average ability.

"I guess I learned the importance of fundamentals back in Little League," says John. "My dad was the manager of our team, which was sponsored by the Art Compton Cleaners in Terre Haute, Indiana. We learned that it was fun to do things the right way. No fooling around! For instance, Dad used to lay the shin guards on the infield about ten feet up each base line, and we would practice bunting at those shin guards. Any time a bunter would hit one of the guards he'd get an ice cream cone!"

The rewards for proper execution of fundamentals have changed for Tommy John. A pitcher who can bunt well in the big leagues can become rich and famous.

"Another thing I learned when I was ten years old was the proper way to throw a curve. The Philadelphia Phillies had a minor-league farm team in Terre Haute. They were managed by Bennie Bengough. I had read Bobby Feller's book *How to Pitch* and I thought I was able to throw a Bobby Feller curve! My dad asked Bengough to look at my curve and he helped me learn the right way to snap it off. Most kids never learn the proper snap, so they hurt their arms. I threw only three or four a game in Little League, but they were the right curves and they didn't bother me."

Tommy was a winning pitcher and a good hitter right on through his high school career. After graduation he signed a contract with the Cleveland Indians. Later he was assigned to the Dubuque club of the Midwest League. Tommy was so impressive that the Indians brought him up to Cleveland to pitch in an exhibition game against the Cincinnati Reds, a team that was on its way to winning the National League pennant.

"I really didn't know what pitching was all about till that game!" recalls John. "I could see then that I had a long way to go to become a big leaguer."

Tommy spent the next two seasons learning his craft. Dividing his time between Charleston, West Virginia, in the Eastern League, and Jacksonville, Florida, in the International League, he won 23 games and lost 20. But he struck out twice as many batters as he walked, and the Indian management was convinced that he had mastered the difficult art of control. Left-handed pitchers who, at the age of 20, can get their good pitches over the plate are rare.

Late in 1963, John was promoted to the Cleveland club. But his record of two wins and nine losses the following year was not impressive. Sam

McDowell, Tommy's roommate at Jacksonville, was more to the Indians' liking.

When the Chicago White Sox asked that a young left-hander be included in a three-club trade that was being set up by Cleveland, Chicago and Kansas City, Tommy John became a member of the White Sox pitching staff. (In that trade Kansas City sent Rocky Colavito to Cleveland; the White Sox sent Jim Landis, Mike Hershberger and Fred Talbot to Kansas City; and the Indians gave up Tommy Agee and John Romano, as well as Tommy John. In time John proved to be the best bargain.)

At Chicago, Tommy became a pupil of Ray Berres, one of the best pitching coaches in the business. Berres was an excellent analyst of pitching problems. He asked only one thing of his pitchers— that they demonstrate control. To Berres, control was a matter of confidence and rhythm.

Pitchers who lack confidence are generally afraid that they can't throw the ball over the plate, or afraid that if they do get it over, the batter will clobber it. Tommy John had plenty of confidence, but his rhythm was not always as good as it had to be.

"Berres taught me the importance of pitching rhythm," says Tommy John. "I used to hurry my delivery and try to throw the ball too fast. Berres called me a 'rush artist' and we worked constantly on keeping my delivery smooth."

John's fast ball was not particularly swift, but it did sink fast when it reached the plate. If he rushed his delivery his elbow would be out ahead of his body as he came through, causing the ball to stay high instead of sinking.

"It was perfectly logical," says John. "You release the ball high and it will stay high. When my rhythm was good the ball would do what it was supposed to do. Since I didn't have overpowering speed at any time I had to make the pitch sink in order to be effective."

Tommy's rhythm was so consistent in 1965 that

Fellow Little Leaguer Bill Freehan steps on John's shoulder while trying to prevent a runner from stealing second base. John had fallen to the ground after taking a fierce swing at the ball.

he led the White Sox in wins and strikeouts. His record of 14–7 and earned-run average of 3.08 was as much as any pitching coach could ask from a 22-year-old. Ray Berres gave his young student straight A's in pitching education.

"Proper rhythm isn't hard to learn," says John, "but it sometimes is difficult to maintain. It helps to have a coach keep at you. He can see when you lose your rhythm quicker than you can feel it. Of course, when your rhythm is off the batters usually let you know it pretty quick, too!"

Tommy had even less trouble with hitters in 1966 than he had had in his first winning season. He opened the season with a victory over California, beating the Angels, 3–1. John thus became the first pitcher to win a ball game in the new stadium at Anaheim.

During the month of May he pitched two shut-outs, beating the Tigers, 1–0, and the Yankees, 2–0. Two months later he shut out the Yanks again for his ninth win of the season. And in August, with his fast ball sinking and his curve snapping off sharply, John won four games, including his fifth shutout, this time over the Indians, who had once owned his contract.

Although John won only one game in September, it was a sparkling 3–1 victory over the Baltimore Orioles, soon to be crowned the World Champions. During the season he won two out of the three games he pitched against the Orioles. That year he wound up with a 14–11 record, and his 2.62 earned-run average ranked him fifth in the American League.

John's 28 victories in two seasons with the White Sox had made him a popular success with the Club management. Tommy was also a favorite with Sox fans. His big grin and friendly personality made a hit with everyone.

"I guess you'd have to call me an extrovert," says Tommy, "I like people. I like working with people. In fact, I think I'd like to be a coach some day and work with young pitchers."

To the amazement of White Sox manager Eddie Stanky, Tommy asked if he could attend the instructional camp to be held in Florida by the Sox after the season ended. Stanky thought that it was unusual for a 23-year-old to display such willingness to help other young pitchers, especially when it could be pointed out that John's instructions might enable some other youngster to take his pitching job!

When the 1967 American League season got under way, the White Sox were once again thought of as potential pennant winners. No other team in the league had such powerful pitching. For the first two months Joel Horlen and Gary Peters were practically unbeatable. The Sox bull pen was superb in relief. The Sox leaped into first place on June 11 and stayed there for 62 days.

But the White Sox couldn't hit. As a team they batted .225. One run was considered a White Sox rally. Two runs meant a big inning!

Like most teams, the Sox had a "hard-luck pitcher," for whom they scored few if any runs. For several years Joel Horlen had been the unfortunate member of the Chicago staff. In 1967 it was Tommy John. He found that if he didn't pitch a shutout himself, he would often be shut out by the opposing pitcher. Grimly determined, John made as few mistakes as possible.

"During the stretch where I had five shutouts in eight starts," says John, "I pitched as well as I ever could hope to. I had complete confidence in myself. I had good stuff throughout each game. My rhythm was consistent and I must have averaged no more than ninety-five pitches a game."

One doesn't have to be a mathematician to know that a pitcher who throws fewer than 100 pitches a game makes very few mistakes. John was clearly at the peak of his form. Then the virus hit him and he was stopped cold.

"When you lose twenty pounds in a couple of days it takes a lot out of you. Since it happened in the middle of the summer there was no chance I could gain much of that weight back. So I was pretty weak whenever I went out on the mound."

Manager Stanky tried to save Tommy's strength as much as he could. But the White Sox needed a shutout daily, so John took his turn. As the pennant race entered into the last two weeks of the season, Tommy did his best to keep Chicago in contention. At Fenway Park in Boston he shut out the Red Sox with what Stanky called the finest pitching under pressure that he had ever seen.

But even near-perfect pitching couldn't carry the Sox all the way. On September 29 they faced elimination from the race. John had to beat Washington to keep the Sox alive. He made a heroic try, holding the Senators to one unearned run, which turned out to be the only score of the game. Chicago was out of the race.

Where luck is concerned, a pitcher has to take the bad with the good. Tommy John, a graduate student in the pitching art, learned that hard lesson in 1967. In the future, with his health restored and his rhythm and confidence assured, he could expect to have fortune smile on him once again. He, above all, could afford to say:

"Wait till next year."

Index

Numbers in italics indicate photographs

Aaron, Hank, 74
AAU, 119, 123, 128
Adcock, Joe, 74
AFL, 44
Agee, Tommy, 164
American Association (baseball), 6
American League, 6, 7, 10, 12, 15,
  17, 23, 24, 27, 101, 102, 106,
  107, 152, 156, 167
American Legion baseball, 104
Atlanta Braves, 78
  See also: Milwaukee Braves.
Auerbach, Red, 54

Baltimore Colts, 39, 46, 49
Baltimore Orioles, 3, 81, 109, 166,
  167
Banks, Ernie, 86, 87
Bannister, Roger, 125
Baseball Hall of Fame, 107, 151
Baugh, Sammy, 43, 137
Beckert, Glenn, 89
Bengough, Bennie, 162, 163
Berra, Yogi, 102
Berres, Ray, 164, 166
Boston Celtics, 54
Boston Patriots, 44
Boston Red Sox, 4–8, 9, 10, *11,*
  12, 13, 15, 17, 23, 27, 109,
  112, *113,* 156, 169
Bradley, Bill, xi, xii, *52,* 53–62, *63,*
  64, 65, 66, 67
  as All-America, 53
  as College-Player-of-the-Year, 53
  as Little Leaguer, xi, xii, 56
  as high school player, 56, 57
  as Rhodes Scholar at Oxford, 55,
    61, *64,* 65, 67
  in Fellowship of Christian
    Athletes, 60

in Holiday Tournament, 61, 62
in NCAA Tournament, 62–64
in Olympic Games (1964), 59–61
quoted, 55–58, 65, 67
records of, 54–56, 58, 59, 63
style of, 53–55, 57–61, 63
training of, xii, 55–57, 60, 67
values of, xii, 55–58, 60, 61, 65,
  67
with N. Y. Knickerbockers, 65
Brooklyn Dodgers, 20
  See also: Los Angeles Dodgers.
Buhl, Bob, 71
Bukich, Rudy, 35
Bunning, Jim, 150
Burdette, Lew, 71
Burleson, Dyrol, 129, 130

California Angels, 25, 156, 157,
  166
California League, 91, 92, 94
Carolina League, 6
Cepeda, Orlando, 96, 112
Charleston, West Virginia (minor
  league baseball club), 163
Chicago Bears, 29, 31, 33, 35, 36,
  44–46
Chicago Cubs, 81, 83–87, 89, 91,
  92, 94–98, 104
Chicago White Sox, 12, 13, 24, 156,
  159, *160,* 161, 164–169
Cincinnati Reds, 3, 6, 71–78, 153,
  163, 164
Cincinnati Royals, 64
Clemente, Roberto, 96
Cleveland Indians, 17, 20–27, 102,
  104, 105, 163, 166
Cochrane, Mickey, 151
Colavito, Rocky, 164
College All-Stars (football), 144

Compton Relays, 129, 132
Conerley, Charley, 141
Crandall, Del, 18, 19, *24, 72*
Cunningham, Glenn, 133

Davis, Willie, 32, 33, 144
Dean, Dizzy, 17
Denver, Colorado (minor league
 baseball club), 149
Detroit Lions, *47,* 49
Detroit Tigers, 13, 17, 25, 148–157,
 160, 166
Ditka, Mike, xii, *28,* 29–32, 33–*34,*
 35–37
 as All-America, 29–31
 as All-Pro, 29
 as high-school player, 29, 30
 as Little Leaguer, xii, 29, 30
 as Rookie-of-the-Year, 36
 at University of Pittsburgh, 29,
 31, 34, 35
 injuries of, 30, 33
 quoted, xii, 29–31, 33–37
 scoring of, 35, 36
 style of, 31–37
 training of, xii, 31, 35–37
 values of, xii, xiii, 29–31, 33, 34,
 37
Dressen, Charlie, 151, 152
Dubuque, Iowa, Club, 163
Durocher, Leo, 86, 89, 92, 94–97,
 99

Eastern League (baseball), 163
Elliot, "Bump," 149

Feller, Bob, 17, 162
Fellowship of Christian Athletes,
 48, 60, 140
Fisher, Jack, 87, 109
Freehan, Bill, *146,* 147–*150,* 151–
 155, 156–157, *165*
 as high-school player, 148, 149

 as Little Leaguer, 148
 at University of Michigan, 149
 batting average of, 149, 151, 152,
 154, 157
 home runs of, 151–154, 157
 injuries of, 153, 154
 in minors, 149
 quoted, 147–156
 RBI's, 153, 157
 records of, 149, 152, 156
 style of, 148, 149, 151, 153, 154
 training of, 148–154
 values of, 154, 155
 wins Golden Glove award, 152
Frick, Ford, 107

Gibson, Bob, 112
Graves, Ray, 141, 142
Green Bay Packers, *32,* 144
Grelle, Jim, 130, *131*
Grissom, Marv, *160*

Haines, George, 118–120
Hannum, Alex, 54
Hefferle, Ernie, 31
Heisman Trophy, 137, 143, 144
Herman, Billy, 8, 9
Hershberger, Mike, 164
Hill, Harlon, 36
Hodges, Gil, 15
Holtman, Ken, 94
Horlen, Joel, 159, *160,* 167, 168
Hornsby, Rogers, 107, 108
Houk, Ralph, 106
Houston Astros, 78
Houston, Texas (minor league
 baseball club), 83
Howard, Bruce, 160
Howard, Elston, 102
Hundley, Randy, 95

Iba, Hank, 60
Ilyichef, Leonid, 121

International League, 21, 22, 163
International Swimming Hall of
  Fame, 115

Jacksonville, Florida (minor league
  baseball club), 22, 163, 164
Jay, Joey, xi, xiv, *68*, 69–*72*, 73–*76*,
  77–79
  as All-Star, 73
  as Little Leaguer, xi, xiv, 69, 70,
    75, 79
  earned-run average of, 78
  in minors, 70, 71, 78
  quoted, 69–71
  records of, 75
  style of, 70, 72–74, 78
  training of, 70, 71, 78
  values of, 70, 74, 75
Jazy, Michel, 132, 133
John, Tommy, *158*, 159–*160*, 161–
  165, 166–169
  as high-school player, 163
  as Little Leaguer, 162, 163
  at Indiana State University, 159
  injuries and illnesses of, 159, 161,
    165, 168
  in minors, 163, 164
  quoted, 159–168
  records of, 166, 167
  style of, 162, 164–166, 169
  training of, 161–165
  values of, 161, 162, 167
Johnson, Lou, 98
Johnson, Walter, 17

Kaline, Al, 156
Kansas City Athletics, 102, 105,
  164
Keino, Kipchoge, *135*
Kennedy, Bob, 85, 87
Killebrew, Harmon, 15
Korneyev, Yuri, 60
Koufax, Sandy, 17–19, 26, 27

Lakeland, Florida (minor league
  baseball club), 21
Landis, Jim, 164
Lary, Frank, 149
Lipon, Johnny, 22
Little League, Inc., xi–xiv, 5, 19,
  20, 29, 42, 56, 69, 70, 73–75,
  79, 82, 89, 90, 104, 117, 125,
  130, 131, 140, 148, 149, 162,
  163, 165
  aims of, xi
  criticism of, xiii, xiv, 69, 70
  World Series of (1948), 69, 79
Lodi, California (minor league
  baseball club), 91, 92, 94
Lonborg, Jim, 27
Los Angeles Dodgers, 73, 78
  See also: Brooklyn Dodgers.

McCarver, Tim, 112
Macaulay, Ed, 67
McDowell, Sam, xi, xii, *16*, 17–*21*,
  22–*24*, 25–27, 163, 164
  as high-school player, 19, 20
  as Little Leaguer, xi, 19, 20, 27
  injuries of, 21, 22, 25–27
  in minors, 20–22, 163, 164
  pitches of, 17, 18, 21, 23–27
  quoted, xii, 17, 19–23, 26, 27
  records of, 17, 19, 23, 25–27
  style of, 17–24
  training of, xii, 19–23
  values of, xii, 18–20, 22, 25–27
Maloney, Jim, 73
Mantle, Mickey, 3, 4, 102, 103,
  106, 107, 108
Marchetti, Gino, 39, *40*, 41, 46
Maris, Roger, xi, xiii, *100*, 101–*103*,
  104–*106*, 107–110, *111*, 112–
  113
  as high-school player, 104
  as Little Leaguer, xi, xii, 104
  batting average of, 101, 105, 108

home runs of, 102, 105, *106*–110,
111
injuries and illnesses of, 102,
105, 107, 110, 112
in minors, 105
quoted, 101, 104–110, 113
RBIs, 102, 110, 112
style of, 102, 105, 108, 110, 112
training of, 105, 110
values of, 101, 109, 110, 112,
113
wins Most Valuable Player
award, 102, 103, 106
Martin, Billy, 12
Mathews, Eddie, 74
Michel, Tom, 42
Michelosen, John, 31
Midwest League, 163
Milwaukee Braves, 6, 70, 71, 72,
73, 74
See also: Atlanta Braves.
Minneapolis, Minnesota (minor
league baseball club), 6
Minnesota Twins, 12, 13, 15, 17,
21, 156
Minnesota Vikings, 39–41, 44–46,
48–50
Monday, Rick, *150*
Moses, Wally, 152–154
Mossi, Don, 150
Mulvoy, Mark, 8
Musial, Stan, 4

Namath, Joe, 137, 141
National Basketball Association, 55,
65, 67
National Collegiate Athletic
Association, 53, 58, 62, 63, 64
National Football League, 29, 31,
35, 36, 39, 44, 46, 48
National League, 12, 71, 73, 74, 81,
86, 92, 112, 156, 163
New York (baseball) Giants, 89

New York (football) Giants, 36, 49–
51
New York Knickerbockers, 54, 55,
61, 64, 65, 67
New York Mets, 77, 87, 97
New York Yankees, 17, *21*, 74, 101,
102, 105–110, 153, 166
Nitschke, Ray, *32*
Nye, Rich, *88*, 89–92, *93*, 94–99
as Little Leaguer, 89, 90
at Berkeley (University of
California), 90
in minors, 91, 92
quoted, 89–92, 94–99
style of, 89, 91, 92, 94–96, 98
training of, 91, 92, 94
values of, 91, 92, 94, 97, 98

O'Hara, Tom, 130
O'Toole, Jim, 73, *160*

Pacific Coast League, 22, 23, 82
Pappas, Milt, 109
Parilli, Babe, 141
Parnell, Mel, 23
Perry, Ray, 91, 92, 94
Pesky, Johnny, 7
Peters, Gary, 159, *160*, 167
Philadelphia Eagles, 35
Philadelphia Phillies, 72, 78, 79,
162
Philadelphia 76ers, 54
Pittsburgh Pirates, 18
Pizarro, Juan, 71
Portland, Oregon (minor league
baseball club), 22
Portsmouth, Virginia (minor league
baseball club), 79
Pyle, Mike, 35

Raleigh, North Carolina (minor
league baseball club), 6
Roarke, Mike, 150

174   INDEX

Robertson, Oscar, 53–55, 61, 63,
64
Robinson, Brooks, 81
Robinson, Frank, 3
Romano, John, 164
Rookie League, 91
Rose, Murray, 119, 120
Russell, Cazzie, 61, 62
Ruth, Babe, 101, 107–110, 113
Ryun, Jim, xi, *124,* 125–*128,* 129–
131, 132, 133–*135*
as Little Leaguer, xi, 125, 130,
131
as photographer, 133
at University of Kansas, 131, 133,
134
breaks four-minute mile, 129,
131, 134
in Olympic Games (1964), 129–
131
quoted, 125, 127, 128, 130–135
records of, 126, 128, 131–*135*
training of, 126–129, 131, 134
values of, 126, 127, 131, 132
wins Sullivan Award, 134

Sain, Johnny, 157
St. Louis Cardinals, *8, 14,* 97, 110,
112, 113
St. Louis Hawks, *66*
Salt Lake City, Utah (minor league
baseball club), 21
San Antonio, Texas (minor league
baseball club), 83
San Francisco 49ers, 144, *145*
Santo, Ron, *80,* 81–*84,* 85–87, 89
as All-Star, 86
as Little Leaguer, 82
as Chicago Cubs team captain, 87
batting average of, 84–87
home runs of, 84–87
injury of, 87
quoted, 81–87

records of, 81, 87
style of, 81, 82, 84–86
training of, 83–85
values of, 81, 82, 85–87
wins Player-of-the-Year award, 87
Scheffing, Bob, 150
Schoendienst, Red, 112
Schollander, Don, xii, *114,* 115,
116, 117–*121, 122,* 123
as Little Leaguer, xii, 117
at Yale, 123
in Olympic Games (1964), 115,
116, *116,* 119, *121,* 122, *127*
in Olympic Trials (1964), 118,
120
quoted, xii, 116–123
records set by, 115, 118–120, 123
style of, 118, 120, 121
training of, xii, 116–118, 121, 122
values of, 116–121, 123
wins Sullivan Award, 122
Scott, George, *113*
Seattle Rainiers (minor league
baseball club), 82
Shannon, Mike, *8*
Sherman, Allie, 50
Sisler, Dick, 112, 113
Snell, Peter, 131, 132
Southeastern Conference, 43, 138,
141–143
Spahn, Warren, 71, *72,* 73
Spurrier, Steve, *136,* 137, 138, *139,*
140–*143,* 144–*145*
as College All-Star, 144
as high-school player, 140, 141
as Little Leaguer, 140
at University of Florida, 137,
138, 141–144
in Fellowship of Christian
Athletes, 140
quoted, 138, 140, 142–144
records of, 141
style of, 140, 142

values of, 140, 144
wins Heisman Trophy, 137, 143, 144
with San Francisco 49ers, 144, 145
Stallard, Tracy, 109
Stanky, Eddie, 12, 156, 167–169
Stengel, Casey, 102, 108
Strickland, George, 26
Sullivan Award, 122, 134
Swift, Bob, 150

Talbot, Fred, 164
Tarkenton, Fran, 38, 39, 40, 41, 42, 43–46, 47, 48, 49, 50, 51, 60, 141
  as All-America, 43
  as Little Leaguer, 42, 43
  at University of Georgia, 43–47
  in Fellowship of Christian Athletes, 48, 60
  injuries of, 44, 50
  passing of, 39, 40, 44–46, 47, 48, 50
  quoted, 41–46, 48, 49, 51
  style of, 39–42, 44–46, 48–50
  training of, 45, 46, 48
  values of, 41, 43, 45, 46, 48, 50, 51
Tebbetts, Birdie, 24, 25, 26
Terre Haute, Indiana (minor league baseball club), 162
Texas League, 83
Timmons, Bob, 125–128, 131
Triandos, Gus, 150

Unitas, Johnny, 137

Van Breda Kolff, Bill, 58, 62
Van Brocklin, Norm, 41, 45, 46, 48, 50, 137
Veale, Bob, 18

Wade, Bill, 31, 32, 36
Washington Redskins, 43, 44
Washington Senators, 15, 24, 169
Weismuller, Johnny, 123
Whatley, Jim, 43
Wichita, Kansas (minor league baseball club), 70
Willey, Carl, 74
Williams, Dick, 10
Williams, Ted, 4, 5, 6, 13
Wynn, Early, 25

Yastrzemski, Carl, xi, xii, 2, 3, 4, 5–8, 9, 10, 11, 12, 13, 14, 15
  as high school player, 5, 6
  as Little Leaguer, xi, xii, 5
  awards of, 4, 6, 15
  batting average of, 6, 7, 9, 13, 15
  home runs of, 7, 9, 11, 12, 13, 15
  injuries of, 9
  in minors, 6, 7
  in 1967 World Series, 13, 14
  on All-Stars, 7, 10, 12
  quoted, 5, 6, 8, 9
  records of, 7, 9, 12, 13, 15
  style of, 3–6, 9, 10
  training of, xii, 5, 7, 10
  values of, xii, 6–10
York, Rudy, 106

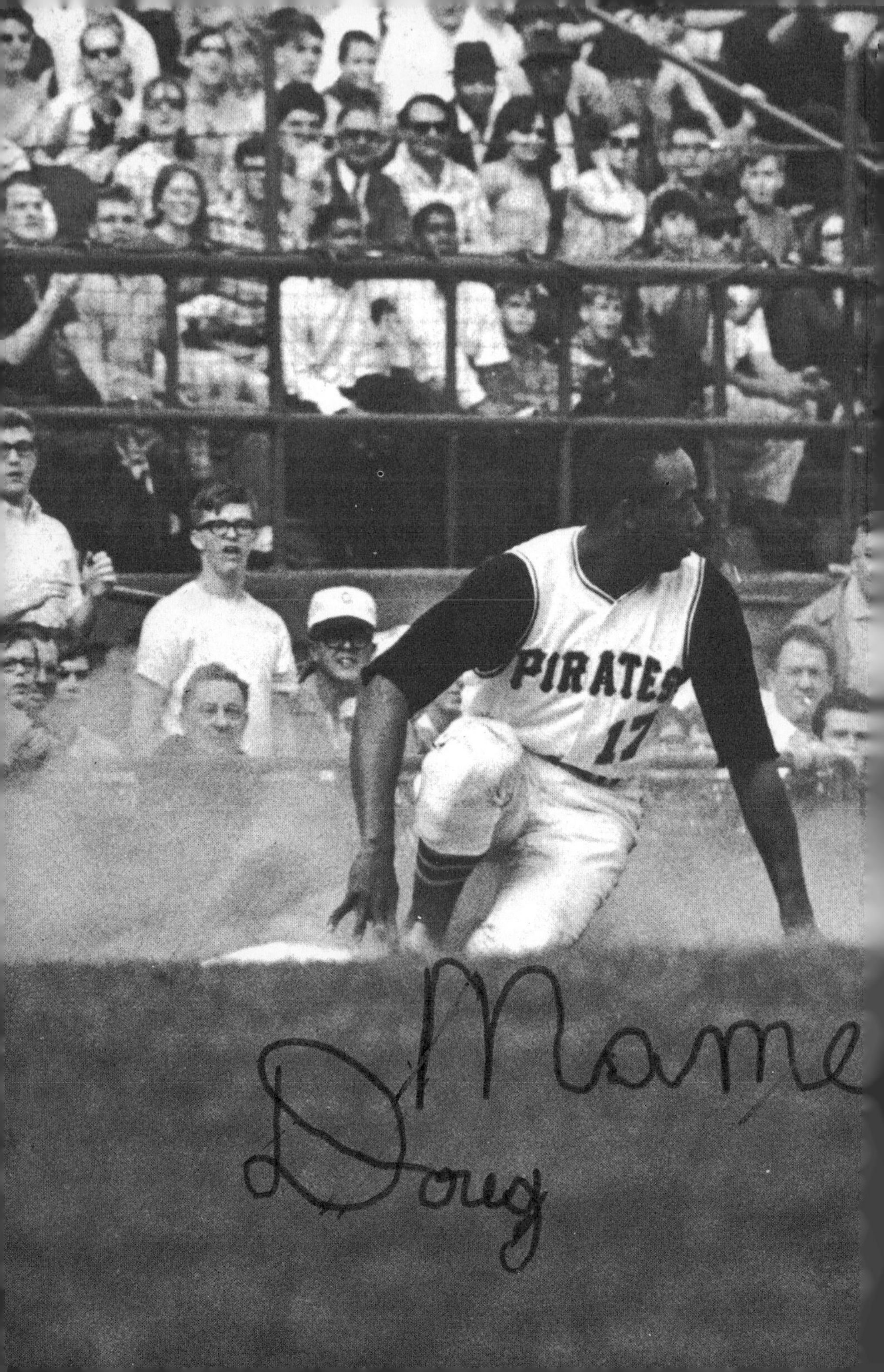
PIRATES
17